FIRST CHUR
7899
Fred

DADDY'S HOME at LAST

DADDY'S HOME at LAST

What It Takes for Dads to Put Families First

MIKE SINGLETARY
with Russ Pate

ZondervanPublishingHouse
Grand Rapids, Michigan

A Division of HarperCollins*Publishers*

Daddy's Home at Last
Copyright © 1998 Mike Singletary and Russ Pate

Requests for information should be addressed to:

ZondervanPublishingHouse
Grand Rapids, Michigan 49530

Library of Congress Cataloging-in-Publication Data

Singletary, Mike.
Daddy's home at last : what it takes for dads to put families first / Mike Singletary with Russ Pate.
p. cm.
ISBN: 0-310-21569-2
1. Fathers—Religious life—United States. 2. Fathers—United States—Psychology. 3. Fatherhood—Religious aspects—Christianity. 4. Father and child—United States. 5. Family and work—United States. I. Pate, Russ. II. Title.
BV4529.S45 1997
248.8'421—dc221 97-40093
CIP

This edition printed on acid-free paper and meets the American National Standards Institute Z39.48 standard.

All Scripture quotations, unless otherwise indicated, are taken from the Holy Bible: New International Version®. NIV®. Copyright © 1973, 1978, 1984 by International Bible Society. Used by permission of Zondervan Publishing House. All rights reserved.

Sonya Bemporad, Zig Ziglar, Anthony Evans, James Dobson, Norm E. Evans, and Bill Glass are quoted by personal, written permission.

All rights reserved. No part of this publication may be reproduced, stored in a retrieval system, or transmitted in any form or by any means—electronic, mechanical, photocopy, recording, or any other—except for brief quotations in printed reviews, without the prior permission of the publisher.

Interior design by Jody DeNeef

Printed in the United States of America

98 99 00 01 02 03 04 /❖ DC/ 10 9 8 7 6 5 4 3 2

To our fathers

CONTENTS

INTRODUCTION

Ironically, this project did not start within the framework of a book about fatherhood. We initially planned to draw on my experiences as a motivational speaker and consultant in the areas of corporate leadership, teamwork, and cultural diversity to produce a manuscript designed to energize the American workforce.

I especially wanted to share insights into the systems and processes by which companies and executives that are headed sideways or south can move up to the next level.

During the course of our collaboration, however, as we focused on factors that shape and define success in the business world, we began relating those same factors to family life. The connections came easily and naturally, because qualities that enable businesses to thrive are the same that allow families to grow and prosper. There's a great overlap between the paradigms for success in either arena. Even multinational companies operating on a global basis must employ the same principles of family as medium-to-small businesses or mom-and-pop shops. Principles such as:

- having a crystalized vision;
- exercising strong leadership;
- establishing clear communication;
- developing teamwork and a commitment to one another;
- sharing a winner's attitude.

Success begins at home, not away from it. I don't believe an individual can be whole or complete—or become one of society's so-called "winners"—without having the foundation of a strong, healthy home life. Otherwise, success will be temporary and transitory. Or illusory.

We pushed our motivational book to the back burner as this project about fatherhood and, by extension, parenting, began heating up. We chose the title *Daddy's Home at Last*, in part, because it's an everyday expression to which many readers can relate. Countless times in countless families the magical cry "Daddy's home!" has reverberated through the household, resonating with joy and delight. Sadly though, for many youngsters in the 1990s, that oft-heard jubilant refrain has been supplanted by a muffled and forlorn question: "Where's Daddy?"

Our subtitle, *What It Takes for Dads to Put Families First*, sounds a cautionary note. It's time for a major change in the behavioral patterns of dads and dads-to-be who define themselves by conquests and achievements outside the home. Those men must set a new agenda; they must understand their ultimate rewards will be realized by becoming loving husbands and nurturing fathers.

When you examine problems that afflict our society, it's not difficult to trace many of them to the fracturing, or fragmenting, of the family unit. And, in many cases, this fracturing has occurred because daddy's not home.

What qualifies me to write a book on fatherhood? Not necessarily the fact that I'm the father of six young children. Or the fact that I'm the product of a broken home, someone who can speak firsthand about a child's feelings of despair and abandonment when divorce stands your whole world on its ear.

Not necessarily the fact that together with my wife, Kim, I have structured my career as a motivational speaker around the needs of my family. Or the fact Kim and I frequently counsel and pray with married couples on parenting and relationship issues.

Not necessarily the fact, either, that I address many of the themes in this book in my frequent presentations to churches, Bible study groups, or organizations such as the Fellowship of Christian Athletes (FCA) and Professional Athletes Outreach (PAO).

What qualifies me to write this book is a combination of all those experiences, plus a heartfelt desire to be of service to my fellow man. I'm eager to help sound the alarm for American men who have drifted away from, or rejected, their responsibilities as family leaders.

Do I know all the formulas for successful fatherhood? No, of course not. However, I do understand the dynamics of growth and change, and I believe those dynamics can be applied to fatherhood. In other words, successful fatherhood can be anticipated, executed, managed, and evaluated.

Although the title, *Daddy's Home at Last*, might seem to imply that this is a book written exclusively for males, that's not our intent. This book is addressed to all family members. It's a book written for young men and women contemplating marriage, as well as couples contemplating starting a family.

It's also a book aimed at helping parents, or prospective parents, get on the same page in their approach to raising children. It spells out some of the pitfalls and provides solutions to problems that inevitably arise.

Some fathers answer the rhetorical question "How do you know if you're doing a good job as a parent?" by asserting: "Give me twenty-five or thirty years and I'll tell you then. Let me see what kind of job my kids do with raising their kids, and I'll let you know."

Bzzzz, wrong answer.

Dads need to know today, right this minute, how we're doing as parents. We need immediate feedback that tells us our children feel safe and secure and that they are filled with self-esteem and confidence. Dads need to know our children have dignity and self-respect. We need evidence that our children exercise discipline in all facets of their lives.

To the extent that daddy's home, and fully involved in the parenting process, that feedback will likely be positive.

But if daddy's presence at home is primarily ceremonial, if he behaves like a despot or an autocrat, or withholds his love, he runs the risk of losing his wife and children. At that point, he will have failed in his principal calling: extending God's kingdom.

Dads must bring all the energy and creativity they can to parenting. Don't let male pride, ego, and tradition ruin your family before it's had the chance to flourish. Guide your family, not with your own principles, but with God's. Count on his grace and wisdom to sustain you.

Be prepared to face adversity in fatherhood. You'll be tempted to stray off the path. Your own children will test your resolve.

But don't surrender in the face of a challenge. Never, ever, give up. One of my favorite Bible verses, James 1:12, says, "Blessed is the man who perseveres under trial, because when he has stood the test, he will receive the crown of life that God has promised to those who love him."

American families need the leadership of real men. Men who understand that fathers must be servants to their families. Men who are transparent, vulnerable, and not afraid to say "I love you." Men who are not afraid to admit their mistakes. Men who treat their wives and children like gold.

American families need real men who base their leadership principles on the greatest leader of all: Jesus Christ. Husbands who will work together with their wives to lead children through a morally chaotic time.

If we as dads can show our children that we are men of God, and live that example every day—falling down as we will, but by God's grace getting up and moving on—we have the chance to make a tremendous difference in their lives.

In the end, dads have the opportunity to leave our children something far more precious than money. We can present for their acceptance the security and peace of mind that comes from knowing that by grace we are saved and that by faith we will be received.

As a dad, that's the greatest gift I have to offer my children.

—MICHAEL SINGLETARY

CHAPTER 1

A Question of Balance

Among problems confronting America today, one of the most serious, with the most dire and lasting consequences, is the breakdown of the family unit. And families, in the majority of cases, have become fractured, split, and twisted horribly out of shape because daddy's not home.

He's either away on a business trip or working late at the office. He's gone to the country club to sharpen his golf swing or he's meeting his buddies at the local bar for drinks after work. Maybe he's meeting with a headhunter about a new career opportunity or doing some industry networking that might lead to an attractive job offer.

Perhaps daddy had to take his best clients to the Bulls game or the Cubs game or the Bears game or the Black Hawks game. There's always a game going on, no matter what time of year, which explains why some men tend to regard ESPN sportscasters as members of their extended family.

None of these choices are bad in and of themselves. But if dad's actions are not balanced against his children's needs, if they do not meet family rules and guidelines and, most critically, if they don't have mom's support and consent, dad's decisions about where and how he spends his time can deal a crushing blow to his family.

I know all about the time crunch dads face. As a corporate consultant and motivational speaker, I constantly face agonizing decisions about time management. Virtually every time I drive to O'Hare Airport in Chicago, on my way out of town for another speech or seminar, I'm tempted to ask: Should I stay or should I go?

A huge part of me wants to remain at our home in the Chicago suburbs with my wife, Kim, and our six children—Kristen, Matthew, Jill, Jackie, Brooke, and Becky. I desperately want to be at home with my family, to help Kim with the daily chores, to greet the older children when they come home from school and to spend the evening hours attending to our children's needs, whatever they may be.

That's not always possible, of course. My speaking schedule is such that I'm forced to spend more time away from my family than I would like. Which explains why I am conscious of making the most of the hours we're together and why I am committed to being home in spirit even when I have to be away physically.

Crunch Time

After my retirement from the Chicago Bears in 1992, as I began sorting through business opportunities associated with beginning a second career, I began traveling frequently. At some point, Kim, my darling wife, whom I married in 1984, realized that she had become angry and frustrated by being left home alone with our children so often. When Kim confronted me about her feelings, I registered my surprise.

"I hear you, honey," I told her, "but don't you see that I'm doing all this for you and the kids? I'm trying to give us security for the future. If you think I enjoy being away from the family so much, you're mistaken. It eats a hole in my heart."

Kim wasn't buying any of that. "Don't get hurt patting yourself on the back so hard," she said. "We don't need this big house and all the other stuff, Mike. What we need from you as a husband, father, and leader of this family is your presence and commitment. What we need from you is *you*."

Kim's stinging words filled me with shame. She forced me to take a closer look at our family situation. Our children were starting to grow up, developing their own personalities. They were full of energy, enthusiasm, and wide-eyed curiosity. They were also asking Mommy questions about where Daddy had gone and when he'd be back home.

I could see the concern reflected in Kim's beautiful green eyes and hear it in her voice. "I appreciate what you're trying to do for us, Mike," she said, "but you have to realize I can't raise these children alone. You talk all the time about wanting to have a great family, but just exactly how do you suppose that will that happen if you're not here for date night or family night or to pray with our children? We need you here for family meetings, to help with homework, and to help resolve conflicts. How are you going to manage to do all those things when you're not at home?"

I stood mute, at a loss for words.

"We're going to have to sit down together and work out a reasonable schedule for your business travel," she said. "Either that, or this family will probably become just another statistic, another casualty of neglect."

D.O.A. because Daddy's Out Again.

"You know I'd never let that happen to us," I interjected. "You and our children are the most important things in my life."

"Well, maybe you should start demonstrating that in a different way," Kim concluded. "And just remember this, Mike, everything else has a price, but time cannot be negotiated."

By traveling so extensively and trying to keep so many business deals going, I had allowed myself to get caught up in trying to meet society's definition of success. Not our own.

Kim and I have worked together closely ever since to conduct business with a minimum of stress and strain on our children. Kim helps me schedule appearances and coordinate travel plans so that I spend the fewest possible number of nights away from home. Even so, I probably sleep in a strange bed seventy-five or eighty nights a year. That's too often.

I've come to realize how important it is for parents—especially dads—to slow down. The time crunch we all face as dads needs to be dealt with by putting family issues before career issues. We have to focus on our children's needs and address their concerns. We need to reclaim them from the streets and back alleys, the shopping malls and video arcades, before it's too late.

Getting My Priorities Straight

I lacked a sense of balance about fatherhood in the early years of our marriage. As defensive captain of the Chicago Bears, I enjoyed a reputation throughout the National Football League for intensity on the field and single-mindedness of purpose off the field.

I was consumed with being the best middle linebacker in pro football. No one in the league watched more film or spent more time studying other teams' formations and tendencies. That passionate preparation helped bring me plenty of personal recognition (numerous All-Pro honors and Pro Bowl appearances), but, as I know now, it came at a price.

Too often I shut myself off from Kim and our kids. While she was having to deal with crises and put out fires, I was down in the basement lifting weights or watching game film. When Kim needed my help with some problem or situation, likely as not I would bury my head in the Bears' playbook and shout, "Can you do that, honey? I'm busy right now."

That pattern of behavior is not something I'm proud of.

Fortunately, I had married a remarkable woman who would neither accept the role of football widow nor put up with an absentee husband. She helped me strike a balance between my obsession to achieve greatness as a football player and my role as husband, father, and family leader.

Kim had heard me speak many times about the value of family and the critical need for fathers to express their love for their children. One day, out of the blue, she told me, "Mike, you talk a lot about being a good father, but you're not exactly living up to that standard."

"What do you mean by that?" I demanded to know.

"When you're home, you're not home," Kim said. "You bring your work home with you and use it as a shield. Either you keep the kids away from you by saying you're too busy to play with them, or you stay away from them. You have been shutting the children out of your life, Mike."

Kim was right—as usual. I was shirking my responsibility to serve the needs of our children. I had been keeping the kids at arm's length so as not to disrupt my preparation for Sunday's game. Kim made me see that my priorities were out of whack. Over time, with her help and plenty of prayer, I was able to change.

Falling into a Routine

Having daddy home, though, contributes little to a child's development and self-confidence if dad's unable or unwilling to do more than just be there. Dad has to represent more than a large body lazing around on the couch or recliner, reading the newspaper or fiddling with the remote control. He has to be more than someone who brings work home from the office and retires to the study and shuts the door, as I did.

Kids are savvy. They have built-in antennae as sophisticated and highly calibrated as any radar screen or strategic defense scanner. You can't fool them. They know if your mind is back at the office, thinking about tomorrow's meeting or next week's agenda. They know if they have your undivided attention or if you're just paying them lip service.

Before Kim brought me to my senses, I was one of those fathers unable to make the kind of emotional investment that parental love demands. I was guilty of being selfish, of doing my own thing. Everything in our household, or so I imagined, centered around my being able to gear up to be a genuine "Samurai" (my nickname with the Chicago Bears) on Sunday afternoon, firing up my teammates and rocking Soldier Field with big hits.

Today, I would caution fathers not to let their home life become a routine. I fell into that trap. So did my father.

Charles Singletary worked, came home, ate dinner, and went to bed. That pretty much summed up his existence for the years we lived together before he moved out: work, home, dinner, bed. My father preached in the Pentecostal Church on Sunday, but the other six days of the week he followed the same schedule.

His life was as predictable as the sunrise. By rigidly following his routine, Dad paid hardly any attention to his wife and kids. He seldom joined in nightly conversations with my mother and me. He rarely planned any family events out of the ordinary. He said he was too tired to come watch me play football games.

"Rev" was a hardworking man in his construction business. I can close my eyes and still see the sweat pouring off his face and glistening on his large muscles. I can still hear him yelling "Get me the pick" or "Get me the shovel" or "Get me the hammer." Those memories remind me of the story about the rural youngster who showed up at school for the first day of class in the first grade. When the teacher asked him his name, he replied, "Gitwood."

I may not be a genius, but I am smart enough to know that there is more to life than working, making money, sending your kids to school, retiring, and then dying. There are huge gaps to be filled, and how you choose to fill them determines, in large measure, the quality of a dad's life.

I appreciated my father for his efforts to provide for our family, but I wish he could have found balance in his life. For many years, Dad's world revolved around his job and his crew, not his family. Because of decisions he made back then, I have had to work hard in recent years to renew a relationship with him. Although I love him and respect him as a father, we have struggled at times to have meaningful conversation.

I never want my own children to feel that they have to work hard to cultivate a relationship with me. Daddy's love will be a constant in their life.

A Constant Tug of War

I went overboard with my zeal for football. My dad got carried away with his construction business. I cite those examples because any man seeking to be a good father—or even a great one—needs to rearrange his priorities and better manage his schedule to maximize family time.

Working with corporations on issues such as leadership, teamwork, and cultural diversity, I've met countless executives who express concern over their family situation. These people bring me in to explore ways in which they can take their company to the next level. Or they seek my counsel on how to crystallize a corporate vision or define a mission statement that will get everyone in the company on the same page, pulling together.

But invariably, in private conversation, many of these same executives tell me that the demands of business have created pressure points and tension within their family. It's a constant refrain.

They admit to a tug of war between their responsibilities at work and at home. They are wracked with guilt about their inability to strike a balance that would permit them to have good feelings about their performance in both arenas.

Work or family? Family or work? Which one should get the emphasis? Typically, when the chips are down these fathers choose to put business considerations first and family matters second. "I'll make it up to my family later," they pledge with every noble intention. Yet, as job demands continue to expand, make-ups become harder and harder to reschedule. Many never happen.

Last fall, for example, I met with an executive for a Chicago-based freight company about a possible consultancy. Before we had proceeded very far with the discussion of what type of motivational role I could fill for the company, he began telling me about his personal life.

He was in his early thirties and had two young children at home. He recognized they were in the most formative period of their lives. He knew he should become an active participant in their development. In fact, he spoke movingly about how much these children needed him to be active in their growth.

But this man was also a rising star in the company, and he knew his performance in the short-term would be critical to his climb up the organization. This man could envision his career ascending, but he realized one trade-off for advancement would be long hours away from home.

"It's an impossible position to be in, Mike," he said, pouring out his frustration as tears welled up in his eyes. "It's a real dilemma. What would *you* do?"

"It's not impossible," I responded. "Like any other decision you face, it only involves making a choice. That choice is yours alone; no one can make it for you. But since you asked, if I were you, I would put the needs of my family first."

That may not have been the response he wanted to hear. He never contacted me again after our initial meeting. I didn't begin a consultancy with his company, so I can't confirm whether he's still grinding away at the office, giving his family short-shrift, or whether he's been able to strike a better balance.

But I pray it's the latter.

I'm reasonably sure that many dads suffer such pangs of remorse about being away from their family. That's an important starting point: before you can deal with a problem you must be aware one exists.

Raising an issue, however, isn't the same thing as resolving it. By talking about the need to be more committed fathers, but taking no corrective action, some dads are no different than the cigarette smoker who insists he will quit any day now—then lights up another Marlboro or Kool.

Men and women can apply the same methods they use every day in their business careers to solve parenting problems. They can begin by analyzing what action needs to be taken and what options are available. It's generally a good idea to be flexible in your approach and willing to experiment and fine-tune. It's also best to exercise patience, because change usually doesn't occur overnight.

I have a good friend who's been facing a dilemma with his twin sons. They're nearing adolesence, the age when boys naturally tend to get rambunctious. My friend makes a ninety-minute daily commute from his home into metropolitan Chicago, which means he faces three hours on the highway, Monday through Friday. He leaves his home by at least 6:30 A.M. and generally doesn't get back until 8 P.M.

That leaves precious little time for parenting, so the burden of keeping up with two high-powered boys going at one hundred miles an hour falls mostly on mom. At times, she feels overwhelmed.

My friend, his wife, and the boys are addressing the situation. They've identified dad's work-related absence as the primary problem they face as a family. They are weighing such alternatives as relocating closer to his work site or moving his work closer to their current home. Whatever the outcome, he has identified the immediate need to become less of an absentee father. He plans to assume a larger role in his sons' lives.

My friend is one of millions of men who realize that it's time for daddy to come home, where he's needed most. These men recognize the value of making decisions within the context of putting family considerations first.

I'm greatly encouraged that many dads have decided to renew their commitment to fatherhood and are coming home. Home to stay.

CHAPTER 2

What It Takes to Put Family First

I like the phrase "family first" as a motto for the growing awareness in America that fathers need to start rebuilding the family unit. The motto suggests a shared attitude about addressing the needs of our spouses and children ahead of our own.

But family first shouldn't be interpreted to mean "family only." Human beings aren't meant to live isolated lives. We need to interact with others. One of the main themes Kim and I stress to our children is maintaining great passion for your personal pursuits and great compassion for others. We are all part of a larger family called humankind.

No Stalking the Sideline

Some people who followed my career in professional football made the mistake of assuming that I would remain connected with the game. I've heard many people speculate—in the media, as well as directly to my face—that one day I would become head coach of the Chicago Bears and carry on the tradition of some great leaders like George Halas and Mike Ditka.

That's flattering talk, but such a possibility never entered into my thinking. In fact, football was one of the career choices that I immediately ruled out once I hung up the cleats and shoulder pads for good.

Please understand, some of the finest men I've ever met are football coaches. I'm deeply thankful they encouraged and motivated me and brought out my best effort. Some of my best friends—men and women—are working in the coaching profession right now.

Unfortunately, though, the sports landscape in America has changed dramatically—and not for the better. In college athletics, alumni pressure is so intense that coaches have to focus on winning, not on building character, or teaching morals and ethics, or seeing that student-athletes graduate on schedule.

At the pro level, the vast sums of money from broadcasting rights' fees and multimillion-dollar contracts have changed the dynamics of the game. Team owners now get involved in decision making and exercise their formidable egos. A "win—or else" attitude permeates professional sports.

I heard an NFL official say recently that to win a championship now takes twenty-four-hour-a-day preparation. That's an overstatement, but not by much. As a result, it's virtually impossible these days for a football coach to have a family life.

Sorry, stalking the sidelines isn't for me. My family comes first. If I'm going to devote twenty-four hours a day to being a coach, I'll coach my own kids, thank you.

I could cite several examples of coaches who let their need to succeed on the football field render them failures as husbands and fathers. A Super Bowl championship and a big diamond ring are hollow symbols of victory if they come at the expense of loving relationships at home. Unfortunately, you could fill an address book with the names of football coaches who failed to put their family first—and in the process paid a considerable price.

I'm not suggesting it's impossible to be a successful football coach *and* a good father and family man. My coach at Baylor University, Grant Teaff, who now is the president of the American Football Coaches Association, has managed to fill both roles admirably. So have other coaches at the high school, collegiate, and professional levels.

Coach Teaff, together with his wife, Donnell, and their three daughters, was an inspiration to me from the moment I arrived on the Baylor campus in Waco, Texas. When practice was over, when the pads and helmets had been put away and the socks and jocks were being washed, Coach Teaff went home to his family. When you him saw out in public, either at a university function or during his leisure time, you always saw Donnell (and frequently his daughters) at his side.

What I witnessed in Grant Teaff—a loving husband and father with deep religious convictions—was an example that I wanted to emulate. The qualities Coach Teaff possessed stamped him as a success, regardless of his win-loss record in football—which happened to be a pretty darn good one.

What It Takes

Growing up, however, most boys lack the wisdom and foresight to realize that being a good family man, like Grant Teaff, should be one of our primary goals in life. That's not one of the lessons we typically learn.

Instead, we are taught how to stand up for ourselves, how to defend ourselves, how to protect our turf. We're taught how to build things like model race cars and airplanes, bait a fish hook, shoot a rifle, change the oil, and clean out the carburetor. We're taught how to play sports and exploit our physical prowess.

My father taught his sons all about being physical. We learned how to swing a sledgehammer and an axe. We learned how to handle a jackhammer to break up concrete. My dad helped us build our bodies into impressive specimens, but he neglected to help us develop our emotional cores.

I have an older brother named Charlie. He inherited my father's ability to fix things. Replace the tube in the television? No problem. Put the antenna on the roof? A snap. Something clogging up the dishwasher? Let me see it. Air conditioner's not working? It's a breeze.

Charlie's one of those mechanically gifted guys who can break things down and put them back together. He has the gift. What he hasn't always had is peace of mind. There's a large part of him that's unfulfilled. He struggles with many personal problems. His heart is heavy. He needs reconciliation with his self.

I'm happy to say that the last time I visited him in Houston, he was making great strides. Charlie has stopped playing the classic role of the victim, and he's begun to take responsibility for his own success and failure. He's moving forward with his life.

What Charlie and I—and the rest of my brothers—failed to learn growing up was what constitutes a real man. I've vowed not to let that ignorance be passed on to the next generation.

Being a Real Man

One day last year I was talking to Matthew and I asked him, "Remember what we were talking about the other day? What did Daddy tell you about what it takes to make a real man?"

"I don't know, Dad," he responded.

"Sure you do, son," I said. "Just think about it for a minute. Try to fill in the blank in this sentence: A real man is ________."

After a pause, Matthew proclaimed, "A real man is someone who loves his family."

"Okay, that's good," I told him. "Now, what are some of the other qualities of a real man?"

His eyes lit up as another idea popped into his head. "A real man is someone who keeps his word," he said. He was cooking.

"What else?" I asked him.

"A real man obeys God," he finally said.

"That's great, son. Now, can you think of anything else that makes up a real man?"

"Uh, let's see," he said, going down the checklist. "A man loves family, obeys God, keeps his word . . . uh, I guess, a man works hard."

"That's right," I said. "He honors his body, mind, and heart. He works his hardest and does his best, no matter what he's doing."

Matthew looked at me like he was expecting a lecture. I prefer to think of these conversations as teaching, not lecturing, but my delivery still needs some work.

"That's the entire list, son," I said. "Those are the four qualities that make a real man. And whatever else you do, I want you to remember those things."

I'm trying to teach my son that being a real man has nothing to do with being rich or famous. I want Matthew to realize that a real man doesn't have to own his own company, drive a luxury car, walk around with a thick money clip, or have a gorgeous woman on his arm. Being a real man has nothing to do with macho things like wearing gold, talking trash, being full of shuck-and-jive.

By the same token, I frequently talk to my daughters about what it means to be a real woman. And, as with my conversations with Matthew, I stress the same four points: a real woman loves her family, obeys God, keeps her word, and works her hardest.

There's something else I tell the girls. "Sweetheart," I tell each of them, "you need to spend as much time with your mommy and your grandmothers as you possibly can. You need to be with them, go places with them, be in their shadow every time they move. Your mother is the epitome of what a great woman is all about. If I were you I'd ask her so many questions about life—'Mom, what about this?' or 'Mom, what about that?'—and take advantage of this opportunity. Because there will come a time in your life when she's not around, or can't be there, and you'll have to rely on the wisdom that she's shared with you."

If my daughters walk in the steps of their mother, they will learn about the integrity and character of a real woman. And, to the extent I can impart lessons to them as their father, they will learn enough about the nature of men, and the human heart, not to choose as a life partner the kind of man that cannot give them true love.

One of these days, my daughters are going to be asking me about boys. And a few years later, they're going to ask me what kind of man makes a good husband.

I can't wait to have those conversations. I'll tell my daughters to find a man who stands on his own two feet. A man who puts God first in his life, and who loves them the way that Jesus loved the church: devotedly and unconditionally.

I'll tell them to find the kind of man who doesn't substitute style for substance. A man who knows his responsibilities and carries them out. Someone who won't, when the chips are down, fold up and run out.

That's not a real man. That's a façade.

Confusion About Daddy's Job

There seems to be confusion among some parents about what exactly *is* daddy's role in a family. Is he supposed to be the breadwinner, the provider of food and shelter? Is his principal job to protect the family from harm? Or is he supposed to be the hunter-gatherer who goes off and attains glory for the family name?

Some people might insist fathers are supposed to be all three things, and perhaps more.

I believe that daddy's primary function is to empower his children by investing in their physical, emotional, and spiritual maturity. Along with mommy, daddy needs to build in his kids the self-esteem and self-confidence that will equip them to face any challenge or stare down the fears that paralyze so many lives.

I've heard young fathers ask, "What is it that I'm supposed to do? There aren't many how-to books for dads."

Sure there are. The Holy Bible, for one. The Scriptures make it clear that fathers are supposed to serve their families and bring along the next generation of human life. Fathers should also serve as role models for their children.

What many dads fail to grasp is the concept of service. They believe a family's primary purpose is to fill *their* needs and cater to *their* whims. With such a selfish attitude, they are doomed to be failures as fathers. Their actions will uproot marriages and families like twisters ripping across Tornado Alley. Society will be forced to clean up—or cope with—the debris these dads leave in their path.

The Enemy

Anyone who seeks to become a good father and family man must first overcome the principal enemy: selfishness. I know, I've been a selfish father. I've also grown up as a member of the "Me" generation and I've seen where our selfishness has led.

It's appalling. We now have men going in every which direction, doing their own thing, looking out for themselves with little consideration or compassion for anyone else. Over the past two decades, we have witnessed a phenomenal rise in the number of deadbeat dads who have abandoned sons and daughters and who owe millions in child support payments, not to mention alimony.

Society counts among its ranks fathers who have never bothered to marry the mother of their children. At the opposite end of the spectrum, there are men who show disdain for the sacredness and sanctity of wedding vows by getting married a handful of times.

I sometimes think selfishness has caused more devastation in this country than all the earthquakes, hurricanes, blizzards, and other acts of nature.

If you're a family-oriented father, however, you will change your focus 180 degrees, from me to *we*. You will structure your schedule, gladly and willingly, around your children's activities.

Let me give you an example: I have out in the garage a new set of Wilson golf clubs. These are beautiful clubs, which I received as a gift for playing in a celebrity pro-am tournament. They've only been out of the box twice, or maybe three times, in the two years I've had them.

Why? Because we have six children in our home, that's why. I'd rather be with my kids than out on the golf course. I realize golf is a popular sport among businessmen and athletes and—with the arrival on the PGA Tour of the phenom Tiger Woods—it's catching on with youngsters, too. But until or unless my children take up golf, those handsome Wilson clubs are going to be left out in the garage, gathering dust. As anyone who has played golf with me can attest, perfecting the golf swing is not one of my top priorities.

The Payoff

What's the payoff for being a good family man? That is, the kind of father who puts his family first?

For starters, the products of a stable, loving, and caring home environment are likely to be children with a good self-image. Kids who are solid young citizens are less likely than others to use drugs, commit crimes, or run afoul of the law.

Kids brought up in caring, nurturing homes are also more likely to value education and pursue degrees beyond high school. They are more likely to open their hearts to the truth of God and thereby develop honesty, loyalty, respectfulness, and obedience.

Beyond that, I believe that if children witness a loving relationship between mom and dad, and if what parents say is consistent with what they do, America's kids will have the chance to change the world. Because their lives will have such profound meaning and impact, our children can grow up to become true difference-makers.

They have the potential to become the kind of people who move society forward.

CHAPTER 3

Forgiving Daddy When He's Gone

Daddy can't be a family leader or a leadership partner with mommy if he allows his focus to drift from what's going on at home. Daddy can't mail in his participation as a parent, either—he has to be actively involved.

Along with mommy, daddy needs to teach, guide, and instruct his children, doing so with as much patience, wisdom, and care as he can possibly muster. Dad should be generous with his hugs and kisses and vocal with encouragement and praise. The tone and manner he uses in conversation with his children should empower them and engender in them feelings of self-worth.

Daddy's divorce from his family creates a deep and empty pit. Long-term, children can more easily cope with daddy's death than his desertion. Death is permanent; desertion might be open-ended. If daddy walks out the door, there's a chance, however remote, that he might walk back in.

Josh's Story

As we were beginning this project, we watched a segment on *20/20*, the weekly ABC-TV news program. The piece vividly told the story of a ten-year-old boy named Josh, who's growing up in a single-parent household. His mother,

Kathy, had ended her relationship with Josh's father before she knew she was pregnant. Josh has never even met his dad.

Despite his mom's best efforts to provide a positive and loving family environment, Josh feels an emptiness inside because daddy's not home. Josh told the interviewer, John Stossel, that he wanted his father around so they could do "guy" stuff together. His dad, however, has taken no role in Josh's development. That decision leaves Josh hurt and confused.

One noticeable aspect of Josh's behavior is his back-talking to his mom. During the program, Stossel cited research that shows dramatic differences in the way kids behave toward their mother, as opposed to their father. One of the first things to decline, when daddy's gone, is the level of obedience and parental respect. At the same time, the level of aggression tends to increase.

Some single moms are able to do a good job of disciplining their children, but many others are unable to cope. The fortunate moms are those able to show respect for their kids and receive respect in return. But that doesn't happen often. And no longer can moms count on getting assistance with discipline from teachers, neighbors, or others in the community.

Disobedience about taking direction and following orders gradually works its way out of the household and onto the playground. Next thing you know, it's in the neighborhood and on the streets. At the root of the problem is a lack of family structure.

The segment on Josh was heart-rending; you couldn't help but feel anguish for this child—and the hundreds of thousands of boys and girls in his situation. Kids left wondering why daddy walked out. Kids who consider themselves unworthy of love.

The segment on Josh brought back memories from my own childhood. I was twelve years old when my father decided to leave our home. That traumatic event would have a profound influence on my life for the next fifteen years—and still does, because it has made me determined to become a great dad.

Although my mother was able to fill an enormous void in my life during the next six years I lived at home with her, I felt vulnerable and confused by my father's abandonment. A large part of me could not let go of the bitter feelings toward his rejection—of my mother, of our family, of me.

My Story

I was the last of ten Singletary children. By the time I was born in October 1958, something of a surprise to my folks, Dad was busy with his construction business during the week and his Pentecostal ministry on the weekends.

My father and I never had a particularly close relationship. I can recall our having only a few heart-to-heart talks. Two of my older brothers, James and Grady, the latter of whom died after an automobile accident in 1971, were much more visible and influential male figures in my life.

But even a dad who is distant and remote like mine, and who basically takes a pass on parenting, leaves a lasting impression on his children. He creates an attitude about security and trust—or the lack of it. Like it or not, dad's imprint is huge and undeniable.

My father did do a good job, however, teaching me about self-discipline and applying myself. He taught all his children about getting the job done and doing it right. He instilled in us a strong work ethic. I'll be forever grateful to him for that.

I'm also thankful for the lessons he taught me about leadership. Though he showed little leadership at home, my dad was a forceful and decisive leader in our community.

He had an uncommon ability to gather the forces, rally the troops, and get things accomplished. He could put together a crew for his construction jobs, and he knew how to get the most out of his men. He had a feel for when they needed to take a water break, or when they needed to push on with the job. He also had a sense about which men in the neighborhood could use a little boost to their weekly paycheck, and he'd round them up for some of his odd jobs. My father would have been a great sales director for some company because he knew how to push people's buttons and get them to respond. He had charisma and flair, which he backed up with hard work of his own.

It made for a winning combination. People in the community respected him. People knew him as someone who kept his word and would do whatever was necessary to see that a job was completed on time and done right.

The Reverend Charles Singletary was a sight to behold in the pulpit. He is a large, imposing figure with a passionate, fiery delivery. As the old church saying goes, he could "preach the kingdom down."

But as a father, this great communicator and motivator was unable to express his love for his children.

Sins of the Father

About two years ago, I accepted an invitation from Bill Glass, the former NFL football star who conducts the Bill Glass Prison Ministries, to speak to a group of female inmates at Cook County Jail in Chicago. The meeting took place in a gymnasium, with the women sitting in the bleachers and the speakers standing at a podium on the basketball court.

I began sharing some personal witness about the troubles and temptations all of us face growing up. I could tell right away that I was failing to connect with the audience. Some of them had a dreamy, faraway expression that told me they had tuned out. Others just glared at me, like I was the enemy.

Which wasn't surprising. One of the prison chaplains had told me beforehand that, because I am a man, these women would look at me suspiciously and contemptuously.

Why? I wondered. Unless they happened to be pro football fans and had heard my name, they wouldn't even know who I was.

"Mike, animosity will arise because you represent the person in their lives who has hurt these women the most," he said.

"Men?"

He nodded. "That's right. Especially their fathers."

The chaplain told me that in his conversations with women prisoners, the one thing they expressed most often was a deep-seated hatred toward men. Virtually all of them had been abandoned, abused, or mistreated in some fashion. Some had been assaulted and battered by their fathers or spouses; some had been sexually molested and raped.

You didn't have to look too closely to see the scars. Their hostility was palpable, as obvious as their prison uniforms. Their faces were drawn; their body language defensive and bitter.

Their cold stares told me the pilot light in their hearts had been extinguished; dads and husbands had blown it out.

"What do you want me to tell you?" I finally asked them, departing from my prepared text. "What if I were your father, husband, or boyfriend? What would you like me to say?"

I suddenly felt the Lord was compelling me to make an apology, or admission of guilt. He gave me the inspiration for what followed.

I walked around from behind the speaker's stand and knelt down in front of them, bowed in prayer. "I'm sorry for what I've done to you," I began, the words coming from somewhere deep inside my soul. "I'm sorry for forsaking and abandoning you. I'm sorry for beating and abusing you. I'm sorry for cheating on you. I'm just so very sorry. Would you *please* forgive me?"

Sniffles and sobs were coming from the bleachers. I kept my eyes closed and continued: "I'm sorry for all that has happened between us. You trusted me. You believed in me. And I let you down. I realize that now. And I know that I was wrong."

Some of the women began weeping uncontrollably. Others were whimpering and mewling, making animal noises that rattled up from their lungs and gurgled in their throats. Such was the depth of their despair. I began crying, too, for all their unmitigated pain.

I cried because these women had been utterly and cruelly betrayed. I knew they would never again believe in handsome princes or knights in shining armor. Their innocence had been stolen. Never again will many of them be able to place their faith and trust in a man.

It's so vital that the first male in a little girl's life—her daddy—be a good role model. He will shape her standards for what a good father and husband is like. In a little girl's eyes, daddy is a god.

These women had had their whole notion about men shattered. Daddy's abuse had created walls of fear and mistrust and barriers to their self-esteem. They had been forced to live their lives within those confining walls, a prison all its own.

My experience at Cook County Jail moved me deeply. Something special had taken place inside those prison walls. I left filled with hope that some forgiveness might actually have taken place. I sensed that some of the bitterness of a few women had begun to subside. These women realized that the daddy who had betrayed them wasn't a god, but just a man. A man with no clue about how to treat a woman, a man with no idea how special women are.

Forgiveness is essential in life. Christ hung on a cross on Calvary so that we would be forgiven for our sins. Forgiveness is the gift he shared with us. When we forgive others, we are free from the bondage of unforgiveness. The person we forgive isn't the only one to benefit from our forgiveness—we do too.

I pray for those women to this day. I pray that they have moved beyond their hurt and found some inner peace. I pray they will seek the Lord's help and find strength to open up their hearts again. I pray they will be able to scale the emotional walls.

I walked away from Cook County Jail wondering how many people in our society are harboring such deep-seated feelings about their fathers. How many of them can't get past the pain daddy inflicted on them?

Daddy's Debris

Several months later, during the summer of 1995, I again joined up with Bill Glass, this time for a prayer session at the Texas state prison in Huntsville, about an hour's drive north of Houston. Huntsville is where hard-timers and lifers serve their sentences.

We spoke to a large congregation, perhaps 1,000 men or more in the prison yard. It was a typical summer day in the Gulf Coast area of Texas, hot and muggy. During my part of the program, I began talking about growing up in Houston, about my experiences as a youngster who made some typically stupid decisions but who, by God's grace, was saved.

I told the prisoners how similar my life had been to theirs, with the primary difference being that I had been able to disengage from a peer group going down a one-way street toward trouble.

"It was making good choices based on a belief system that pulled me away from the bad crowd and kept me out of a place like this," I told them. "I believe that with Jesus Christ you can do all things. I had faith in him and I went forward in my life. Put your faith in him and you can, as well."

Then I introduced the subject of forgiveness and brought the topic around to reconciliation with parents and family. I could tell from the expressions on their faces I'd begun to reach them. The message was hitting close to home.

I told them how I made the mistake of hating my dad for my parents' divorce. And never had I hated him more than when he stiffed me one Christmas.

It was the Christmas (1971) after he'd moved out. Dad asked me what I wanted as a gift and I told him a record player. "Okay," he said, "meet me at Sears on Saturday and I'll get you one."

I took a bus across town that morning and arrived at the store just as it opened. I sat around waiting and waiting. I waited some more, but he never showed up. Late that afternoon, I rode the bus back home—crying all the way. He'd broken his promise. He lied. What was even worse, he wouldn't own up to it the next day. Dad insisted that he'd been at Sears and that he'd gone all over the store looking for me. Then he called me an "idiot" for not being where I was supposed to have been. He tried to lay his guilt off on me. It was the worst, least merry Christmas I can recall.

"How many of you here have that kind of hatred against your own father?" I asked the convicts.

Heads nodded and hands shot up. "Well, I'm here to tell you that you have to find forgiveness in your heart. You can't carry around those bitter, unresolved feelings about your dads, or they'll leave scars on your spirit. You have to get some air on the infection. The wounds have to dry up and heal."

As the meeting concluded, one of the prisoners approached me. He was a Mexican-American, maybe thirty or thirty-five years old, so short that the top of his head came to my chest. He could scarcely speak English. But the tears rolling down his cheeks told me my message about forgiveness had touched his heart.

He started hitting me in the chest. The blows were heavy, as if he were banging into a blocking dummy at football practice or hitting the heavy bag like prizefighters do. A couple of prison guards came running up and tried to grab him and pull him away, but I shooed them off.

"Papa," he blustered. "Papa, Papa, Papa." Every time he said the word, he would thump me again. Bam. Bam. Bam.

I finally gave the man a hug and whispered words of consolation. I could empathize with his anguish. I had shed more than a few tears after my father left our lives.

I would have trouble coming to terms with the void Dad's departure created for our family, and I carried that pain with me for many years. Perhaps I was able to channel some of my anger into cold fury on the football field. Maybe that dark episode in my past added impetus to my motivation to succeed. Looking back now, Dad's desertion might have done some good for my football career.

But for years, all I could recognize was the harm.

Reconciliation Required

It was only after Kim and I married in May of 1984, that she experienced firsthand my sullen and moody side. As she confronted my periods of irritability and non-communicativeness, as she began to delve into the emotional complexities of her new husband, Kim recognized how imperative it was for me to reconcile with my dad.

All through the several years of our courtship, which had begun at Baylor University, I'd been pretty much upbeat and agreeable. Always trying to be on my best behavior and put my best foot forward, always making every effort to be the perfect gentleman around her.

Kim touched such deep and intense feelings in my soul that I willingly opened myself up to her. I allowed myself to become vulnerable. She inspired such confidence and filled me with such a trust that I didn't have to pretend to be anything I wasn't. I didn't have to put on any pretense or act.

Here I was, a strapping football star who devoured running backs like raw meat, but around her I dropped all the machismo and male-ego posturing and simply relaxed. I discarded all the cheap lines I used to toss out to other girls.

I became transparent and let Kim see through me. After our initial attraction broadened and deepened, we began having deep, serious conversations about our possible future together. We talked constantly. We discussed the repercussions of a mixed-race marriage, which were obvious to us both. We were wary of the reaction we'd receive from our parents and families. We were aware that some people at the university and in the community had condemned our relationship. We knew any children our union produced would encounter forms of bigotry and prejudice. Could we withstand the rejection and scorn? Could our kids?

Certainly, we pledged, if we kept our faith and trust in the Lord. We were Christians, we were members of God's flock. We knew God would sanction our union, even if others did not. We had his blessing. We put our faith in the knowledge that what God has joined together, no man can put asunder. As it's written in the Scriptures, "If God is for you, who can be against you?"

Once we were married, we set about being the best couple we could, intent on growing with each other and hopefully growing toward God.

The one unforeseen variable in this ideal scenario was my unpredictable behavior. No sooner had the honeymoon ended than I would inexplicably go off into deep funks and fill the air in our new home with a dense fog of selfishness.

Instead of being open and honest with Kim about my feelings, I suddenly withdrew to myself. When she was critical of something I did, or disagreed with me, I was likely to clam up for a couple of days. Seriously, I might go several days and nights without even speaking to her. I was that immature.

I acted irrationally. I started making excuses for not going to church services on Wednesday night. On other week nights, rather than take Kim to a movie, or out to dinner, I would shut myself up in our basement and study game film.

"Why are you acting this way, Mike?" Kim finally demanded to know. "Where's the man I fell in love with? It's like I'm married to a stranger, someone I don't even know."

"I can't explain what's happening," I snapped back at her, painfully aware of my own immaturity, but powerless to discuss my inner turmoil. "I just need some time to myself. I need some space. Leave me alone."

Deep down I knew the root of the problem. I was being confronted with fear. Fear that I would become the same type of husband that my father had been—moody, sullen, distant, withdrawn, and unfaithful.

Here we were, less than a month into our marriage, and I had already started imitating his pattern of behavior. My actions scared me to my core. I tried praying, but no answer from the Lord was forthcoming. My prayers were being hindered.

Kim and I visited Houston that summer before the Bears' training camp began, and she gained a true perspective on the source of my torment. She observed how I interacted with family members, showing total devotion toward my mother but giving my father, who had moved back into the neighborhood and was living near my mother, the brush-off. The bum's rush.

"Mike, the way you treat your father just isn't right," Kim said to me that first evening in Houston. "He's still your father, no matter what he did to you and your family."

"You don't know what you're talking about," I snapped back at her, barely able to control my rage. "You weren't around to see him in action. He'd leave us for long periods. He would preach in the pulpit on Sunday about sin and evil and wicked ways, and then he'd run around during the week with another woman. What kind of man does that? Not a real man. A phony."

Our trip to Houston had been strained and awkward, even though I'd had the chance to visit with my brothers and sisters, whom I don't see enough, and their kids. I was able to discuss with everyone my dream of opening a family business one day. All the good moments, though, were offset by my edginess from being around Dad.

When we returned to Chicago, I stepped up my workout program in anticipation of training camp. Under Mike Ditka's leadership and with Buddy Ryan's devastating 46 defense, the Bears were becoming a solid playoff contender. We could envision a big season ahead, perhaps even an NFC championship and trip to the Super Bowl. The brass ring was right there in our sights.

I was at my best playing weight, 227 pounds. I had brought my time in the 40 down to 4.6, which meant I could make the deep drops on pass patterns. My arms and shoulders felt like granite. My hamstrings and quadriceps felt like pistons. I was possibly in the peak condition of my entire pro career. In fact, the only muscle that wasn't in prime condition was my heart.

"Don't you see what's eating you?" Kim said one day as she desperately tried to pull me out of yet another funk. "You have to make peace with your father. You can't go on this way. It's tearing you up. It's tearing our family up."

She was right, of course. Kim has this habit of being right about almost everything.

Making Amends

My emotional distress about the relationship I had—or didn't have—with my dad spilled out during an extended phone conversation we had that summer. Kim finally convinced me that I would be unable to grow as an individual, as a husband and potential father, if I didn't make peace with my tormentor.

I picked up the telephone, intending to tell my father that I was sorry for the way things had worked out. But before I could express that thought, my long-repressed pain and anger blew out like a wildcat strike in a Texas oil field. It was a real gusher.

I accused him of being deceitful and a hypocrite, a self-proclaimed man of God who didn't practice what he preached. I raged at him for leaving my mother for another woman and having a child outside our home, for fracturing our family life into little pieces.

Only after I had ranted and raved, my chest heaving at the eruption of emotions, my cheeks covered with tears, my blood pressure shooting through the roof, did I talk about forgiveness.

"Forgiveness?" my father said, sounding like we had developed static on the line and he hadn't heard the word correctly. "Son, why on earth do I need forgiveness from you? Forgiveness for what?"

The line remained silent for several moments. "What am I supposed to say to you, that I'm sorry?" he finally said. "Sorry for what? I did everything I could for you. I kept a roof over your head and food on your table. I tried to do the very best that I knew how. What else did you want from me?"

We went back and forth on the topic of my pain. "Why didn't you spend time with me?" I demanded. "Why didn't you come to my games? Why didn't you tell me you loved me?"

"I was working my butt off for you and the family," he shot back. "What else could you expect from me? I did the best I could. I have no apologies to make to you."

During that phone conversation, I found out my dad had never had anyone in his life sit him down and talk to him about fatherhood. Or about parental love and providing leadership for a family. All he knew was that dads were supposed to work hard and provide food, clothing, and shelter.

He admitted that he had no example of how to be a good father. His own father had been the same way he was: driven, demanding, unable to express any tenderness, unable to create within the family a legacy of love.

I also remember that during the conversation my dad told me that sooner or later I'd realize being a father was not as easy as I seemed to think it might be. After Kim and I began having children in 1985, I realized he was right.

We talked things out for the next couple hours and I felt greatly relieved. Some of the hardness in my heart began to soften. My spirit began to lift, as I felt a sense of peace envelop me. I grew up a lot during that one phone call. I gained wisdom and perspective.

Most of all, I came to the realization that a person can only give to others what he or she has received. Whether it's happiness, hatred, love, or grace—you can only give what you have received.

Unless, that is, you allow God into your heart and allow him to transform your spirit. He can bless you and allow you to move beyond the limitations imposed by your own experiences. With God's grace, a person can give *more* than they've received.

My father had received very little love in his own life. As a boy, he'd been shipped from house to house and relative to relative. He had no manual for parenting to refer to. He only knew about trying to provide materially for his kids; he was clueless about their emotional and spiritual needs.

By the time we hung up the telephone, I felt guilty for never having taken the time to understand why he behaved as he did. I had never known, for example, that his father, my paternal grandfather, had been deserted as a child. And that, at fourteen years old, my grandfather had changed his name from Hildebrand to Singletary.

I had grown up without realizing the generational sadness males in my family have experienced.

For the first time, I began to love my father again. Since that phone call in the summer of 1984, I have felt like a son again, not an outcast. I'm especially grateful that my own children have the chance to have a relationship with their paternal grandfather. Before that phone conversation, I would not have foreseen that happening.

Although it would have been wrong and unjust, I probably would have wanted to shield my children from my father. Hate can do that; it's a powerful emotion. Fortunately, however, love is an even stronger one.

My new relationship with my father would not have been possible without forgiveness and reconciliation. If I had allowed my anger to continue, to let my bitterness build a wall around my heart, I could have never again known my father's love. We would have gone to our graves as virtual strangers.

Life is about choices we make or don't make. It's about actions we take or don't take. I know many adults and children reading this book have unresolved conflicts with their fathers. I know many fathers feel estranged from their children.

No matter how your paths diverged, I urge all of you to look within your souls for a way to make peace. If you don't forgive each other and move forward, this bitterness and hatred will be passed along to the next generation of your family—and the one after that.

It's the curse of generational dysfunction.

And I offer this word of encouragement to fathers: It's never too late for you to say, "I'm sorry," to admit your shortcomings and ask for forgiveness from those you've hurt. You can be the one to take the initiative in the healing process. You don't have to wait for your children to come forward.

Will forgiveness be painful? Definitely. Will you have to confront reality? Yes. Will you have to admit your own weakness?

Probably. Will you have to swallow some pride? For sure. Might you be rejected in your attempt? Possibly.

But the suffering in your heart will never go away without forgiveness.

Unforgiven

I have a nephew who's going through some of the same difficulties with his estranged father that I went through with mine. In the summer of 1996, I flew down to Houston to try and help him sort things out. We drove around the old neighborhood for awhile, then went to a restaurant and tried to get to the root of the problem.

"You're never going to feel complete or whole until you make your peace with your dad," I finally said. "Look, that doesn't mean you have to agree with everything that has happened. It doesn't make you any less of a man to say things to him like, 'You know, Pop, you really messed things up. But you know what? I forgive you.'"

My nephew screwed up his face, looking as if he was listening but didn't like what he heard.

"All these frustrations you're experiencing, all the troubles you're having, can be traced back to one simple fact—you're at odds with your father. You're not on the same page. You're not even looking at the same playbook. Look me straight in the eye and tell me that's not the truth."

He sat there in silence, feeling angry without really knowing why. His face was the same one I'd seen many times in a mirror. A face filled with hate.

I'm not sure my words reached my nephew that day. I've heard from my sister that her son has yet to pick up the phone and talk to his dad. Pride and ego stand in the way of reconciliation—and they don't want to relinquish control.

As a result, my nephew still carries around extra baggage. Until he's shed it, he won't be free to become the man he needs to be for his own children. He'll be fighting a battle within himself, a battle he can't possibly win. If he doesn't forgive his father, he runs the risk of redirecting those feelings toward others—including people he loves.

It's a cycle that, sadly, repeats itself over and over.

CHAPTER 4

A Family Reunion

In the fall of 1995, Kim and I traveled back to Waco, where I had made headlines as a three-time All-American linebacker at Baylor University and where we had met one fateful evening at the campus library.

The occasion for our return to Texas was my induction into the state's Sports Hall of Fame. I was honored to be selected to join a distinguished list of athletes and coaches. Texas, it seems, turns out athletes as naturally as Wisconsin turns out cheese.

Two previous inductees, Dallas Cowboys Tom Landry and Roger Staubach, had been my role models in sports. I admired them because on the field they were fiercely competitive and off the field they were strong-minded men of principle and character.

I was excited to be going back to the city that served as the backdrop for my budding relationship with Kim. We had several favorite places off-campus where we really got to know each other, places such as Cameron Park and a favorite picnic spot out at Lake Waco. We also had our favorite hangouts in town like Leslie's Chicken Shack and the Lone Star steakhouse.

A city of 110,000 located on the banks of the Brazos River in central Texas (roughly halfway between Dallas and Austin), Waco is a city with conservative values that reflect the influence of Baylor, the nation's leading Baptist university. On my first recruiting trip there back in 1977, I fell in love with the place.

The folks at the Texas Sports Hall of Fame treated us to a fabulous evening at the Waco Convention Center, including a reception and banquet. I was one of six inductees that night, along with tennis star Tut Bartzen, former Texas A&M football coach Emery Bellard, rodeo world champion Toots Mansfield, LPGA Tour champion Sandra Haynie, and Alabama football coach Gene Stallings.

I had asked Corky Nelson, my old linebacker coach at Baylor, to be my presenter. In his introduction, Corky talked about my intensity on the football field in games and even in practice. My intensity may have seemed a bit uncommon to my teammates and coaches but, trust me, it couldn't hold a candle to his.

I mean, Coach Nelson, who before coming to Baylor had coached the great Earl Campbell in high school in Tyler, Texas, was as intense and focused as any person I know. He could be challenging, intimidating, and humiliating—a real pain in the hip pads, if you know what I mean.

He was in our faces constantly about knowing our assignments and doing drills better. He was demanding and relentless and he could swear better than anyone I'd ever met. It took me several years after I left Baylor to realize what a genuinely decent and caring person Coach Nelson can be. Away from football, that is.

I kept my remarks brief, extending my congratulations to the other inductees (Sandra Haynie and Gene Stallings were unable to attend), thanking Corky and my other coaches for preparing me for a career in professional football, thanking Baylor University for giving me an education (and allowing me to meet Kim), and the citizens of Waco for their continued support.

"Baylor was the start for me of a lot of wonderful things, because of the people who were there," I told an audience of several hundred Texas sports fans. "Coach Teaff was the guy who really taught me a lot about being a man and what it meant to be a Christian athlete."

As I spoke those words, I remembered how Coach Teaff had been one of the people I'd gone to for advice about my deepening relationship with Kim. He had told me that if we truly loved each other and had taken the matter to the Lord in prayer, we should not let society's conventions and mores keep us apart.

"Do what's in your heart, Mike," Coach Teaff told me. "All I can say is that if this involved one of my daughters, I would be proud."

I had the feeling that I probably was the first of his Baylor players who had come to him for a father-and-son talk about interracial marriage. Coach Teaff's response and the stance he took was something I'll never forget.

"If you need me to go see your parents, or Kim's, I'll be happy to do it," he said. "I'm with you all the way."

"Thanks, Coach," I replied. "I appreciate your offer, but we can handle things ourselves." And we did.

I had one other thought to share with the audience that night in Waco, which goes far beyond the scope of celebrity in sports. "I once heard someone say that success really isn't about the awards and all the things we attain in life, although they are very much appreciated," I said. "True success in life is when those people who know you the best love you the most."

Then, looking over at Kim and members of my family, I added, "Tonight I know that, by far, I'm the most blessed individual."

The Texas Sports Hall of Fame induction that Thursday night was a treat, as was seeing a replica of my old Baylor jersey #63 mounted in a large trophy case. Another treat was being honored Saturday afternoon at halftime of the Baylor vs. Texas A&M game. My alma mater gave me a special citation in recognition of my being voted into the National Football Foundation's College Hall of Fame.

It was great stepping out on the field at Floyd Casey Stadium and hearing an appreciative roar from the stands. Some of my defining moments in athletics had come on that field, especially during my senior year, when we became the first Baylor team to win ten games in one season, won the Southwest Conference championship, and hosted Alabama in the Cotton Bowl.

I'm not sure that my presence inspired the Baylor players that Saturday, though, because Texas A&M put a 24–9 licking on the Bears.

The Weekend's Highlight

The best part of the entire three-day trip to Waco came on Friday. To coincide with my Hall of Fame induction, Kim had helped arrange our first-ever family reunion.

My mom and dad came up from Houston. So did most of my brothers and sisters and their children and grandchildren. We had aunts and uncles drive down from Dallas. We had Singletary cousins come all the way from Lubbock, more than 300 miles away.

It was a joyous occasion. The Singletary clan practically filled two floors of the Waco Hilton. For two days and nights, we were practically inseparable, telling tales about growing up, sharing stories of things we'd done together twenty or thirty years ago, seeing family members we hadn't seen in years—or had never even met.

I can't recall a better weekend in my life. The sight of my children playing with their cousins, whom they seldom get to see, filled my heart with joy. The sight of my brothers and sisters with their children and grandchildren filled me with a strong sense of pride. Watching my mother and father watch their offspring, beaming the entire time, made me realize that I'd never seen them so happy. I took in the whole scene and wept unabashedly.

My Uncle Grady made a videotape of our reunion. He went around and asked questions and recorded everyone's responses on camera. I've watched that tape—together with my children—a couple of times since the reunion. I want them to be aware of the continuity of family. I want them to have a sense of who they are and where they came from.

On Friday evening after dinner at the hotel, we had our own revival. We stood together, holding hands, forming a large circle that nearly filled the banquet room and we made a joyful noise unto the Lord. We sang some favorite spirituals like "Amazing Grace" and other Christian songs like "How Great Thou Art."

Fortunately, several Singletarys can carry a tune.

The Singletary Curse

There was a sobering side to all the joy and celebration, however. One of my cousins, David Singletary, addressed the group and began speaking about how the men in our family had been carrying around a curse. The curse of divorce that results from being uncommitted fathers.

David said we needed to turn things around in our lives, take responsibility for our families, be faithful to our spouses, set an example to our children, and get away from the evil paths that had wrecked Singletary homes and disrupted Singletary lives.

The Curse of the Singletary Men. Sounds like a horror or sci-fi movie title, but it does have a basis in fact. The Singletarys have a terrible track record with marriage. All my brothers have been divorced, a couple of them twice. The Singletary women haven't been spared, either: all my sisters, except one, have been divorced. Most of my aunts and uncles have, too.

Our family, like many other American families, has paid a price for not having a loving example in our homes. We've paid dearly for not having a proper role model for fatherhood. The problems go back for generations. My dad's father was abusive to his wife. My father was abusive to my mother. This was the example set for my siblings and me.

It seems to have been a situation where no one in the family ever took the time or made the effort to break the Singletary curse. I feel that with Kim's wisdom, God's guidance, and my mother's prayers, I'm going to get things turned around. I'm going to create a legacy of love within the Singletary family.

Even though I hated my father in some respects for many years, as you now know I picked up the telephone in the summer of 1984 and told him I was sorry for judging him and not being able to forgive him before then. I'll say it again: *You can't go forward in your life with unforgiveness in your heart.* You're going to pass anger and resentment on to your children, and they'll pass it on to theirs.

Some of the women finally spoke up, and began talking about how hard it was to live with a Singletary man. What made it so difficult, they said, was that Singletarys are strong men, but they just don't know how to love. They're too proud. They're too strong-headed. They're too much like Papa John (my paternal grandfather) and his brothers.

After the circle broke up, the men fell mostly silent, while some of the women continued to talk about the Singletary curse. They praised my mother for having had the strength to endure all she had to go through.

Hearing those kinds of comments coming from my own flesh and blood reinforced my commitment to put family first. That's the job for real men: helping shepherd their families through life and providing a strong foundation at home.

Divorce, desertion, and estrangement are not viable options. They don't deserve consideration or mention. Real men take the steps necessary to make relationships work.

I realize, of course, that tensions will arise within families. But much of the pressure comes from the outside. For example, business goes through a downturn and dad loses his job, creating stress and worry. Some men suddenly reach a point where they think they've tried everything possible and things still aren't working out. So they split.

That's not family stewardship or service. That's selfishness. Real men don't run out on their marriages and children.

CHAPTER 5

My Million-Dollar Question

In my second career, I meet many corporate executives on airplanes. Some ask me what I'm doing now that I've retired, but most of them start the conversation by asking about professional football. The three questions I'm most frequently asked are: "Who was the hardest guy to tackle?"; "What is Mike Ditka really like?"; and "Was Walter Payton the greatest running back ever?"

We usually engage in polite small-talk, at which I'm not particularly skillful or adept. I'm more of a straightforward, cut-to-the-chase conversationalist.

When it becomes my turn to ask questions, I'll begin by asking them about their business careers. Some of these men are chief executive officers, some own their own companies, some are sales executives. Others are lawyers or doctors. All of them, by society's standards, are successful individuals.

Then I ask them my Million-Dollar Question: *Are you happy*?

I call it my Million-Dollar Question because if I had a dollar for every one of those businessmen who answered, "No, not really," I'd have enough money to take my whole family to Disney World—and stay in the Orlando area for a month.

You'd think, from a first impression, that these men have things together. They're wearing just the right suit accessorized with the right tie. They have degrees from leading universities. They've sent their kids to the right universities. Their careers have brought them money, power, and prestige. Yet, almost to a man, they confess they have no peace of mind. And the reason primarily relates to their performance as dads.

These conversations, by the way, cut across cultural, racial, and political lines. I remember talking with a gentleman who was the president of a manufacturing company traveling with some of his senior staff members. I asked him how he got started in business, and he told a great tale about how his family didn't have much money growing up, but his father was committed to sending him to college. His father worked two and three jobs at a time, dedicating his whole life to seeing his son make good.

This executive, who was probably in his mid fifties, was pretty spiffed up. He wore his shirt collar open, displaying plenty of gold jewelry. He sported coiffed hair and an overall appearance that told you he was riding high in life.

He told me he was Jewish. I asked him why so many Jewish people are successful in their chosen fields. Does it have to do with work ethic? Is there some secret formula?

"We try to make ourselves indispensable to the community," he replied. "We become bankers or doctors or lawyers who perform a vital role. Or we become independent businessmen and civic leaders. We do those things so our communities can't get along without us."

"What is the strategy behind that?"

"We try to make ourselves indispensable for self-protection and security," he said. "You have to remember that everywhere the Jewish people have gone, we've been chased out."

"Wow," I said, "that makes sense."

This gentleman talked with pride about fulfilling his father's dream, about getting started in business and working and saving until he could start his own company. His manufacturing company had found a niche in the marketplace and established itself as a major force. This man had risen to the next level, becoming a leader in his industry. He was well-respected in his community.

Then I asked him my Million-Dollar Question and watched as his spirits sagged. His mood darkened as if the plane had suddenly moved into a bank of clouds. Not only was he unhappy, he said, but he had a strained relationship with his son, to whom he hadn't even spoken in years.

He turned his head away suddenly. I noticed that he was wiping away tears, embarrassed that I could see him crying. No doubt he erroneously believed that real men don't cry. Take it from me, they do.

"While my son was growing up, I was too busy trying to build my business," he confessed. "I just wanted to be able to give him things I didn't have growing up. And, as result, I wasn't there for him when he needed me. I let him down."

The last thing that executive said was that if he had it to do over, he would make spending time with his son his top priority. From his expression and body language—not to mention his dampened handkerchief—I believed him.

The Yale Grad

On another flight, I visited with a young black man from a middle-class background who had recently graduated from Yale University. He was bright and energetic and enthusiastic about life's opportunities. We talked about his family and when the topic came to mom, his face lit up. He absolutely glowed. When I asked about his father, however, it was as if I had turned off the switch connected to his inner joy. His mood turned somber.

"I don't want to have anything to do with him or his religion," he snapped at me.

Religion? I wondered. What did he mean? I had to draw out an explanation. Begrudgingly, the young man told me his father was a man of accomplishment—a professor of theology, in fact. But his professional success had come at a personal price: he was a victim of alcoholism. "Sometimes, I'd come home and find him passed out on the floor," said the son. "You can't imagine what that was like."

He said his father had never been able to confront his serious drinking problem or the effects of it, which included verbal abuse of family members. Neither had his father ever mustered the strength or courage to apologize for his misbehavior. Finally, his mother had moved out. She just couldn't take any more abuse. The son, too, had decided to walk out of his father's life, leaving the theologian living alone with his hypocrisy.

The young Yale grad also said his father never once uttered the three words he had most wanted to hear while growing up: "I love you."

The Computer Salesman

I also remember being on a flight headed back home to Chicago and visiting with a computer salesman. He was bright and glib, and you could see how he could make a compelling sales pitch. He was one of those kind of guys who could sell refrigerators to Eskimos. When I asked about his family, he proudly said he'd been married for ten years to a wonderful woman, his college sweetheart.

I asked him whether they had any kids, a question Kim has counseled me to stop asking since many couples have problems with fertility and are uncomfortable discussing the topic with friends, much less strangers. On this occasion, I had forgotten her advice.

No, he shook his head.

Well, it's not too late to try, I suggested.

Then the computer guy told me a wrenching tale about how he and his wife had decided not to have children. The reason, he said, was that he was afraid he would become the same kind of dad his father had been.

The computer guy was one of five brothers. Their father had driven them all hard to succeed. But at the same time he was cracking the whip, he withheld any emotional support. The man never told the boys he loved them.

In high school, under the burden of dad's relentless pressure, one of this man's brothers had committed suicide. The tragedy had ripped the family apart. Afterward, his father pretty much packed it in. It wasn't that he was abusive to the family, he simply was never around. The family could not count on him for support. He had surrendered his command as a family leader.

In football terms, he had punted.

The son on the airplane with me had paid a terrible price. He was afraid to start a family of his own because of the sins of his father.

When I think back to that conversation, I can relate the computer salesman's situation to my own life. Thank God, Kim helped me realize I could never become a good father if I went around carrying hatred in my heart for my dad. I had to forgive him for abandoning our family and move on.

I hope the computer guy will one day do the same thing. Forgive his father, move on—and start a family or maybe help some other children who don't have a dad.

Some people might use personal experiences as an excuse not to start a family or commit to parenting. Some might say, "Hey, I'm from a dysfunctional family. I don't need that kind of trouble."

But every family is dysfunctional to a degree (some, obviously, more than others), because there are no perfect people or perfect parents. We all make mistakes and screw up. It's only by the grace of God that we are able to learn from our mistakes, grow and change, and become better parents today than we were yesterday. And better still tomorrow.

I'm looking forward to the day I slide into the seat on a United or American Airlines flight, clasp the seat belt, start a conversation with the businessman seated next to me, ask my Million-Dollar Question and hear someone reply, "Am I happy, Mike? You bet I'm happy. I've got a great wife and family. Here, let me show you their pictures. Boy, am I proud of these kids. They're going great guns. Let me tell you about some of the neat things we're doing together. We're taking a trip to Washington, D.C., next month. Going to tour the Smithsonian Institute and visit the Lincoln Memorial and the Vietnam Veterans Memorial. Tell me, Mike, do you have any children? Aren't kids the greatest?"

A Closing Thought

There was a movie out several years ago called *Field of Dreams,* in which a character played by Kevin Costner feels compelled to build a regulation baseball field in a cornfield on his Iowa farm. Even though the local bank is pressing him and he needs money to avoid foreclosure, he uses valuable acreage to build a ballpark.

Perhaps you remember the movie's theme line: "If you build it, they will come." Costner builds his diamond and all of a sudden, ghosts of famous ballplayers like Shoeless Joe Jackson, who was barred from baseball after the infamous Chicago White Sox scandal of 1919, show up and start playing games.

In the climactic scene, Costner's character finally gets to play pitch-and-catch with his father—tossing around the ol' horsehide—something he had not been able to do as a boy.

The movie brought tears to the eyes of so many of its male viewers that the screenings might easily have been mistaken for pity parties. How many men have gone through life regretting that they didn't get a chance to play catch with their dad? How many dads were too busy to play catch with their sons or daughters, or kick around a football or soccer ball? How many men failed, for whatever reason, to spend enough time with their children?

Please don't get caught in the same trap. Please don't chase the illusion of success outside your family. Otherwise, one day you might find yourself seated next to me on an airplane and hear yourself pouring out a woeful tale about unhappiness and fatherly regret.

CHAPTER 6

A Family Covenant

I speak to people in many enterprises, large corporations as well as small businesses, that express a desire to be better performers in the marketplace tomorrow than they are today. These companies are eager to go to the next level, to become dominant names in their industry. They are seeking my counsel on how to do it.

What I tell them is: "It's fine to talk about greatness or write the word on a blackboard, but believe me, nothing great is going to happen until everyone in the company comes together as one. You have to create a plan, or vision, and everyone—from top to bottom and bottom to top—has to believe in it.

"Talking about being great won't make it happen. Your company has to crystalize its focus on what specific steps are necessary to achieve your goals. Then you must begin taking those steps, one by one. You can't just talk it, in other words, you have to walk it."

Ditka's Vision

Mike Ditka brought that kind of vision to Chicago when he took over as coach of the Bears. He told us exactly what was going to happen—we were going to win a Super Bowl and become world champions. He told us from day one that that was our mission and that, one way or the other, we'd accomplish it. Coach Ditka didn't lie to us; he said we faced an arduous task that would require plenty of blood, sweat, and tears. He also told us the challenge would prove too difficult for many of the guys on the roster, that not everyone would be around by the time we reached our destination.

Coach Ditka began talking title on day one and he never wavered in his approach. Slowly, the Bears players began buying into the plan. We started coming together as a family, and began putting team goals ahead of personal goals and egos.

We began making the sacrifices a team has to make to become a champion. Championship teams require talent, and with talent come big egos; but for a team to be successful, players have to check their egos at the door.

The same changes have to occur in families: parents and children have to focus less on "I" and "Me"—more on "We" and "Us."

A Family Mission Statement

Mission statements are generally associated with large corporations, but there's no reason I can think of for a family not to have one of its own.

At our house, we have a mission statement that our whole family helped devise. We've had our Singletary mission statement engraved on a custom-made piece of oak that hangs in the foyer. Everyone who enters our house can see the sign, which reads:

> "This is the home of champions. As Singletarys, we will always strive to do our very best in all we do. We will strive to be honest and respect each other's feelings, property, and time. We will always pray for one another, fight for one another, and encourage one another. For our trust be not in our home, nor our money or status or knowl-

edge, but in each other, and above all, in our Lord and Saviour Jesus Christ."

What exactly are we saying with our mission statement? One, we are bonding as a family. Two, we are acknowledging that consideration for each other and family camaraderie are primary concerns. Three, we are pledging to place our trust in one other and, ultimately, in Jesus Christ.

From the very first phrase—"This is the home of champions"—we make our ambition known. We want to be a *great* family, not just a good one. We want to be champions in our chosen fields, people who make a difference. Saying so doesn't make it so, because a person's deeds must live up to his expectations, but the positive attitude we express is a critical first step.

This mission statement is the kind of covenant more families could make with each other. It serves to keep all of us focused on our family goals. It helps us set our priorities. It reminds us, should we ever forget, of our relationship with the Lord.

Setting Goals

This may sound unusual, or crazy, to some readers, but our family also sets individual and family goals each year. Around New Year's, we gather as a family and make out our individual lists. Here are some of the goals we set for 1997:

Daddy—Help the children develop; prepare them for teens
Mommy—Focus more on the moment; try to lighten up
Kristen—Have a better attitude; don't be easily influenced
Matthew—Tell the truth; use imagination
Jill—Listen better; be more focused on self
Jackie—Learn how to spell and write her name
Brooke—Master potty training
Becky—Learn to sleep through the night

(Okay, we made up Becky's goals for her. She hadn't yet celebrated her first birthday. But we're fairly confident that if she had been able to talk, that's what she would have said she wanted. For her parents' sake, if not her own.)

Goal-setting is an important exercise for any organization, families included. As the saying goes, if you aim at nothing, you'll hit nothing.

I always encourage people to be target-conscious in everything they do. Keep your eye on the prize, whether it's making an A in school, earning a promotion at work, winning the lead in the class play, having the best piano recital, building the best project for the science fair, or presenting the cleanest uniform in the barracks for inspection.

Goals are great motivators. For example, for each game, the Chicago Bears' defense set goals for turnovers, for limiting opponents to a certain number of total offensive yards, and for stopping any opposing ballcarrier from gaining 100 yards. Meeting those goals week to week helped us achieve greatness overall.

Most companies I've consulted with are pretty good about setting quantitative goals—sales quotas or earnings-per-share benchmarks. But more companies need to set qualitative goals like improving internal communications, fostering diversity and multiculturalism, celebrating victories, and building teamwork and a sense of community.

Dads and moms need to set the same kinds of goals for their family—goals that enable their children to grow together and pull for each other.

The Family as a Team

A family is a team and must think and act like one. On a winning team, everyone has respect for everyone else. Some people call it "chemistry," but I prefer to call it balance. Balance is likely to exist in any organization when leadership is strong, creative, fair, consistent, and smart. Good things happen as a consequence.

One of my favorite sayings about the word *team* is that it stands for "Together Each Achieves More." Sure, it's nice to have superstar talent, but in a heartbeat I'd rather have teammates who flush their egos down the toilet, work selflessly not selfishly, back each other up, brainstorm together, and pick up the pieces without complaint or reprisal or blame when something falls through the cracks.

Show me a team like that and I'll show you a winner.

I particularly remember the great sense of teamwork the Chicago Bears had during our Super Bowl season. Guys would be sitting in the locker room before the game and someone would shout out, "Hamp, you mean so much to me; I'm going all out for you." And Dan Hampton would reply, "Well, watch me out there today, brother. Because I'm playing this one for you."

Another popular saying about the word is "There's no 'I' in team." That means individuals must set aside personal agendas, and suppress any desires to "do your own thing" for the common objective, or overall good, of the group. That's how families should function, too.

A Family Creed

Another form of teamwork Kim and I foster is through teaching our children, as soon as they can talk, to memorize and absorb the words to the Singletary Creed. The Singletary Creed serves as a code of behavior for our family members. It reads:

1—Love Jesus.
2—Love one another.

3—Always obey Mommy and Daddy.
4—Always pray for one another.
5—Put family before friends.

This family creed, like our mission statement, helps define our vision and purpose. It represents a solid seafloor on which Kim and I, and the children, can drop anchor. We will not float away from each other, or the Lord, if we live by this creed.

Time Management

As I mentioned, my business pulls me away from my family more than I would like. Because of that, Kim and I constantly try to get the maximum value out of family time.

We begin most days by praying with our children. Before the older kids leave for school, I read aloud to the whole family, either from the Bible or from a good book. In the evening, we limit TV time and instead talk with each other and play games. Before the kids go to bed, we give hugs and kisses and say prayers together.

Other families no doubt have their own ways of bonding. I suppose many of them ride bicycles together or take walks or play games and solve puzzles. Perhaps they go on picnics or boat rides. Maybe they have hobbies, like singing or dancing or breeding animals, in which the whole family participates. Maybe they simply enjoy sitting around and talking. Whatever they do, they make sure it's done together.

Such moments might seem small and inconsequential to some people. But not to us, or to the millions of other parents who take a similar tack in parenting. By making a full-time, 110 percent investment in our children, we are trying to teach them some of life's most important lessons:

- Because they are God's creations, they are special.
- Their problems are our problems.

- We are a family unit, a team.
- Together, we can overcome any obstacles.
- Daddy loves them, mommy loves them, and, most of all, God loves them.

I know such lessons provide comfort and reassurance to our children, because even to the most well-adjusted and secure kids the world can seem a large, intimidating and pretty scary place. Haven't we all turned off the lights at night wondering if the bogeyman is under the bed, inside the closet, or lurking just outside the window?

I also know from personal experience how important it is for a child to have both parents at home, caring for them, nurturing them, and communicating to them God's love and tender mercy. That's one of the reasons I feel so heartsick for the millions of children who are growing up in single-parent homes. They need both a mommy and daddy in their lives, building their confidence and self-esteem. They need to have exposure to, and experience with, both sides of the male-female equation.

Mr. Mom

Kim, along with her mother and aunt, went on a ladies' retreat to New Orleans last January. That left me in a Mr. Mom role that—thanks to the children's cooperation and assistance—I was able to fill reasonably well.

One day during Kim's absence we got through dinner without incident and went to evening church. During the service, I looked around the congregation and spotted a friend whose father had passed away a few days earlier. After the service, I went over and wrapped him in a big hug and offered my condolences. From the way his body trembled, I could feel his pain. I'm sure he had enjoyed a close relationship with his dad.

When we got home, I fed the kids a snack, changed the baby's diaper, and sat down in a favorite chair. I began thinking about the burdens of my mother and all the single moms who have to do so much each day. Then I began to consider the enormous demands that fall on Kim when I'm away on business and can't help her see to our children's needs.

Suddenly the emotions of the day—from not being together with Kim to sharing my friend's grief—began to overwhelm me. The children, sensing my temporary distress, gathered round.

"What's wrong, Daddy?" they asked.

"At this moment, the picture in my mind is one of my mother, years ago, serving me dinner one night and suddenly breaking out in tears," I told them. "Maybe one of her friends had lost a parent that day, too. I don't know, for sure. But whatever it was, she just started crying. Tonight, I understand why."

My children gave me puzzled expressions.

"Don't worry, Daddy's okay," I assured them. "But I think you've seen today how much we miss Mommy around here. And how much we have to pull together as a family."

That evening, after the kids were in bed, I continued thinking about single parents who are overburdened by daily demands. Just getting to work and getting through a day can be taxing enough; having to come home and pull a virtual "second shift" must be exhausting.

If you are a single parent, I applaud you. I surely don't envy your task of raising your children alone. I encourage you to create some form of family covenant—either a mission statement or creed—to add a little "glue" to help keep your households intact.

Being Together

Let me tell you this: It's hard for a marriage to grow apart or for a family to collapse when dad and mom work together as one. Kim and I are on the same page as parents because we know what the family vision is, we know what the mission statement says, we know what the family goals are. Not the least of which is our being together.

We have constant communication about what we have to accomplish on any given day—what the kids' schedules look like, which church activities are going on, who has to be where and when.

If I'm out of town on business, I may call Kim six or seven times a day, to tell her how much I love her and to hear what's going on at home. I feed off her strength. And, through her, I'm able to keep a finger on the pulse of my family.

I never let myself get too busy to pick up the phone and call Kim to say "Honey, I love you. What can I do for you?" And I'm never too busy to say a prayer for Kim or the kids. I say prayers for them all day long.

I believe that marriage is central to God's plan for the world: Wife has a husband and husband has a wife. Children have both a mother and father. Parents are mentors and teachers and also play the role of heroes. Kids follow their parents' examples and are raised with parental love and affirmation.

When you have those kinds of families—where mom and dad love each other and the kids love each other—you find a powerful team. You have a family that's powerful because it walks together. There's power in the home because God and the Holy Spirit are present there. If you have a bunch of those families in the same neighborhood, you will have a powerful community. There can be no stopping or denying it.

Kim and I also often pray together about our own parenting. We ask God to give us strength and wisdom to discharge our duties to each other and to our children.

"Dear Lord," we'll pray, "help us never take each other for granted or become so busy with our individual pursuits that we neglect family pursuits. Help us be vulnerable enough to always be reaching out to one another. Teach us never to assume anything, and to be honest and open enough to discuss everything with each other.

"Lord, we're depending on you to make us strong together. Amen."

CHAPTER 7

Parental Love and Role Modeling

Children thirst for direction in their lives. At a tender age, children realize they've landed smack dab in the middle of a perplexing and bewildering place. They also figure out quickly they are unequipped to comprehend all its subtleties and nuances. Amid the chaos, they seek order.

Unless they receive guidance, instruction, and supervision from their parents—who play the primary role in shaping their character and outlook—children can develop feelings of inadequacy. They can be intimidated and overwhelmed and lose their self-confidence.

Parental Love

Working together as partners, a father and mother serve as kids' first role models while they discharge their primary duty: providing parental love.

From infancy on, what children need most in their lives is parental love. Kids need to feel special and valued, and they must be grounded in the love of both parents. If only one parent extends his or her love, or if only one parent is present to extend it, kids will feel incomplete—and it shows as they get older.

Mom and dad provide children with a balanced perspective to human relationships. Dads serve as role models for sons. When a boy studies his father, he also learns about the origins of his family and develops an attachment, or bond, to his ancestors. Boys also need to form a close relationship with their mothers to learn that women should be treated with honor and respect. I look at every woman I meet as a mother or sister, someone who deserves my respect.

(How men treat women is one of the key components of character. In fact, one of the criterion I've suggested that my daughters look for in a boyfriend is someone who treats them as well, or better, than I do.)

Girls need moms for basically the same reason boys need dads: to serve as role models. As girls develop a relationship with their father, they learn how to understand men. It's essential that dad shows his daughter love and respect, because by doing so he will raise her standards for prospective life partners.

Together, mom and dad should serve as the family's spiritual and moral compass. They are setting the stage for the next generation. Parents' ability to provide direction for their offspring is related directly to their ability to provide parental love.

What is parental love? I define it as a total, unwavering commitment to nurture the spiritual growth and physical well-being of your children. Parental love is not simply wishing or hoping for the best for them, but actively taking steps to facilitate their development and evolution.

Is parental love expressed by providing your children with a roof over their heads, warm clothing to shield the winter chill, and hot meals three times a day?

No, that's doing the bare minimum, even though by today's standards some might consider it a pretty good job. But it's not enough. Where's the investment of time? The discipline? The support and affirmation?

Is parental love expressed by dressing your children in designer clothes, keeping them shod in the spiffiest athletic shoes, buying the hottest new video games on the market, or giving them the keys to their own car the moment they obtain a driver's license?

No, those things are nice, but kids don't need your *presents*, they need your *presence* and support. Where are the boundaries and standards? Where are the values?

Is parental love expressed by giving children, especially teenagers, carte blanche to do as they please around the house, without curfews, accountability, daily tasks and chores, and without making a contribution to the family's overall welfare? No, that's taking the easy way out. Anybody can give kids what they want. It takes loving parents to give them what they need.

What children need most from their parents is to witness Christian examples of mutual love and respect. Children need to see their parents embody such concepts as honor and character. Through their actions, parents impart these lessons.

By the way, don't expect to receive too much gratitude or appreciation for extending parental love. Instead of thanks, you're more likely to get grief. Only in years to come, when your children have kids of their own and wrestle with these same issues are they likely to thank you for your efforts.

Mom and Dad as Role Models

Parents are the most important role models in a child's life. Parents' role modeling is especially important when the kids are young and impressionable, just beginning to sort out and work through the perplexities and ambiguities of life.

Our patterns of behavior as parents—whether we're generous and giving with our time and attention, how freely and openly we express our love for one another, how firm and consistent we are in establishing family rules and administering discipline—leave an indelible imprint on our children's personalities.

The opinions we parents express, the beliefs we hold, the ideals we espouse, initially become our children's opinions, beliefs, and ideals. If we are positive parents with a problem-solving approach to life, our optimism oozes into their beings. Conversely, if we are negative parents who take a problem-avoiding approach, our pessimism affects their outlooks and personas.

That's why I feel sorry for the children of card-carrying members of hate groups. Before these boys and girls are old enough to think for themselves, their parents feed them a steady diet of exclusion, divisiveness, us-against-them dogma. They are forced to swallow Vitamin H—hatred—in large quantities. Living in homes where shutters are closed and curtains are pulled down to God's loving light, these children have undernourished souls.

I welcome the responsibility of being a role model for my children. In fact, I savor and relish the opportunity. That's one of the reasons why, whenever possible, I take one or more of our kids along with me to business meetings.

Such occasions afford us quality time together. The kids can see how to act, how to carry themselves, how to negotiate, how to engage in a dialogue with other adults.

To some, that may sound a bit unusual, but the point is, I want my children with me. I want them to see how I conduct business and relate to other human beings. They can learn from the example I set for them.

"Just sit and listen, watch, and learn," I'll tell my kids. "And if you see me doing something that doesn't seem right, I want you to question me about that, okay?"

I'm not trying to rob them of their childhood. I'm not trying to build a bypass around their teenage years and turn them into mini-adults. That will happen quickly enough. What I *am* doing is trying to steepen their learning curve, to give them a code of conduct they can follow for the rest of their lives.

When I go into a building, I take off my hat. When I greet someone, I give them a firm handshake. When I talk to someone, I look them straight in the eye. When I address someone, I call them "Mr." or "Mrs."—unless they've asked me to call them by their first name.

I don't just talk to my children about behaving in a polite, professional manner. I back it up when we go to a downtown office for a meeting or when we're running an errand at the post office or grocery store. My interaction with others means more to the kids than my words.

Jill's Trip

One platform for role modeling that dads or moms can create for their children is to take them along on a business trip. That gives plenty of one-on-one time in which to teach lessons and learn about needs.

In early 1997, Jill accompanied me on a business trip to Florida. Our third child, seven years old, Jill at times allows her older sister and brother to do her talking for her. She tends to be submissive and fade into the background.

I asked Jill to take charge on our trip, a big responsibility that she stepped up and handled without a hitch. At O'Hare Airport, she picked out our gate assignment from the bank of a dozen or so video screens and steered us through the large crowd. She gave our boarding passes to the gate attendant and found our seats on the airplane.

When we arrived in Miami Beach, Jill checked us into the hotel. When we were settled in, she ordered us a meal from room service.

We had a great time together. When I wasn't tied up with my presentations at the sales conference for Stryker, a medical equipment company, Jill and I were together in our room. We spent an afternoon playing card games, Tic Tac Toe, and I Spy (where you try to guess what object the other person is looking at). We were alone for hours just talking and getting to know each other on a deeper level. I saw a side of my daughter that I would have never seen at home, where she's around her older siblings.

That evening, when I had some free time, Jill and I watched *Pinocchio* on the in-room movie channel. That's a terrific family movie that teaches an important lesson (honesty) about life.

On the way home, Jill again took control of everything. By putting her in charge that weekend, I was helping her spread her wings and fly. You could see her self-confidence soar. In the months and years to come, she'll be able to hold her own if her older siblings try to overshadow her.

My Role Models

The primary role models in my life were—surprise!—my mom and dad. From each I learned valuable lessons that I hope to pass on to my children and *their* children. From each I learned useful skills, an appreciation for God-given talents, a desire to succeed.

I'm not sure enough fathers realize what a profound effect they have on their children's lives. If they did, would they spend so much time apart from their family? I know that men have to work hard to be providers, but if they took a step back and studied how they use their time, they'd realize how ineffective they are with time management and balance.

As I mentioned before, my father taught me the value of hard work and the importance of doing a first-class job in any undertaking. His clients and associates knew they could count on him to deliver a quality product on time. In business, his word was his bond.

Dad also gave me a thirst for knowledge. Though my father only had an eighth-grade education, he was self-educated. He taught me how to think for myself, how to acquire knowledge I lacked, how not to be afraid to ask when I didn't know something. He kept books around the house and made reading an integral part of my life.

From my mother, I learned about feelings for others. About sticking up for the underdog, defending those who can't defend themselves. I learned how to express myself more clearly, and speak with confidence and assurance. She also helped me refine that most underappreciated of skills: listening.

Both my parents taught me about the Creator, about the Scriptures, about the role God plays in our daily lives. They told me stories from the Bible, about people like David, Daniel, Noah, Abraham, and so many others.

They taught me about the courage David showed in facing Goliath and Daniel's faithfulness in entering the lion's den, secure in the knowledge God would deliver him. I learned about Noah's dedication and belief in building the ark and following God's plan. They told me about Abraham's trust when God told him he would bless him (at age ninety-nine) with a son, and how Abraham, at God's instruction, built an altar to sacrifice his son, trusting that the Lord would deliver a sacrificial lamb.

The Ultimate Role Model

This country would be so much better off if fathers redirected some of the enormous amount of time they devote to following sports heroes to learning more about the greatest hero ever. Although, I wish to stress, dads don't really need another hero in our lives. What we need is a Savior.

Which brings me to the ultimate role model for mankind: Jesus of Nazareth. His life on earth is the ultimate standard of everything good. He showed us the way and gave us all that we need to pattern our lives after his example.

Chapter 8

Leadership and Family

Leadership, one of the hottest topics in motivational speaking, is one of my favorites to discuss. Wherever I go around the country, audiences seek insights on the subject.

I've seen some great leaders in action. I've studied the methods of great leaders of the past. Some people have suggested that I possess leadership qualities, as exhibited on the football field for Baylor University and the Chicago Bears. I wouldn't disagree, but I can admit that I wasn't born a leader: I became one.

"Leadership isn't easy," I tell corporate audiences, "but it's no mystery, either. There are no secrets to leadership. Leadership means having the vision to chart the course for a group of people and the courage to make decisions when you face tough times.

"Leadership implies communicating the vision to everyone it affects and getting everyone excited about it. Leadership entails having passion for your particular pursuit and a plan to make things happen."

A Nonstop, Shared Activity

In every family, leadership needs to be a nonstop activity. It's also an activity that should be shared by parents. In our home, for example, Kim and I try to function as leadership partners, or co-chief executive officers.

In an unhealthy home environment, father functions as king, or feudal lord, with everyone else at his beck and call. He's the boss, *numero uno*. What he says goes, and mom and the kids are expected to fall in line, quickly and quietly.

When a man (or in some cases, a woman) rules a family with an iron fist and makes decisions to suit himself, without weighing the consequences for other family members, that's not leadership. That's a dictatorship. Small wonder that, over the years, women become less willing to stay in marriages that seem more like prison terms or indentured servitude than partnerships.

I believe that in a healthy home, mommy and daddy serve as co-leaders. The key words are *serve* and *co-leaders.* Rather than handing down an edict, parents must be willing to serve their children by involving them in the decision-making process. They enthusiastically sell the program *together, as partners,* and get a total buy-in.

(Granted, our children have not reached their teens. Parents tell me that with teenagers, you're more likely to get a tune-out than a buy-in. Kim and I are going to do our best to become the exception to that rule. How? By laying the groundwork now.)

Qualities of Leadership

Whether leadership is applied to family life, business, politics, or sports, it consists of several components: high expectations, consistency, imagination, accountability, empowerment (or giving ownership), accessibility, and visibility. Leadership also implies having the determination to overcome the obstacles that occur in life.

Let's look at each of these qualities.

High Expectations

Leaders set the bar high both for themselves and others. They want to stand out from the crowd, achieve more than the norm, do the best they possibly can in every endeavor. These qualities are the hallmarks of a winner's attitude, which explains why leaders tend to be winners, and why winners tend to be leaders.

People who lead—and by leadership, remember, I'm talking about *service*—must communicate the fact they expect others to be great. But leaders don't ask the people they lead to give more than they give themselves, and they don't set unrealistic goals.

If leaders put the goals too far out, too divorced from reality, frustration sets in. The people they are entrusted to lead will likely give up. They'll flat quit. Real leaders recognize the need to set goals that are both realistic and attainable. They also make sure to celebrate victories, large and small.

One evening at dinner I was talking to our children about setting goals and using visualization techniques to achieve them. "Use your imagination to focus on something you want—making a good grade on a test, scoring a goal in a soccer game, making a perfect movement in one of your cheerleading routines—and visualize yourself doing it," I said. "Make it one of your goals to see yourself doing it."

Matthew said he wasn't sure what goals were, much less how to set them. I was about to explain, when Kristen spoke up.

"Dad, can I tell him?" she asked.

"Sure, honey, go ahead," I said. I was curious to hear what she would have to say.

"Goals are like climbing a ladder," Kristen told her brother and sisters. "Everyone wants to get to the top of the ladder. To get there you take a step and then another step, and before you know it, you've reached the top. Goals are like each of the steps up the ladder."

"That's a really good explanation, Kristen," I lauded her. "Where did you hear that?"

"Don't you remember, Dad?" she said, exasperation creeping into her tone. "You told me that *years* ago."

Consistency

Leaders show consistency in their approach. They are by no means mercurial, prone to fly off the handle or act randomly and capriciously. Nor are they likely to have emotional swings from soaring peaks to deep valleys. Leaders are able to take victory—or defeat—in stride.

Leaders set the tempo, whether at home, in the office, or on the playing field. They come in a variety of types (emotional, quiet, strong, proud, even insecure) but despite their differences in style, temperament, and personality, leaders can be effective if they remain consistent.

Great leaders react the same whether the game or battle—or marketing campaign or product introduction—is won or lost. They are able to draw a distinction between the people they lead and their actions. Say, for example, my children mess up in some chore around the house. As a co-leader of the family, I have to be disappointed in their actions, but not in them.

That's a crucial distinction, one that's often overlooked. Though I may be forced to censure their action (or inaction), I immediately counterbalance my criticism with affirmation and assurance. Maybe I'll hug and kiss them even more than normal. I don't want my children to ever think I've taken my love away. I just make sure that they understand I expect them to make better choices. I'll restate my disappointment in their choices, not in them.

Imagination

Leaders think "outside the box." They are innovative, approaching each new day from the perspective of "What can we do differently?" and "What can we do better?" not "How did we do things yesterday?" They are willing to risk failure if it means that a solution will be found. While never being inattentive to the present, leaders keep looking forward to what can be.

No one is successful without using his or her imagination, without realizing the vast possibilities of ways to do things better. I read a book once about the engineers who developed the steam engine, which led to the development of the railroad system in America. "Why do we need these new-fangled things called 'trains,'" scoffed their critics. "We have horses. We have boats." The people who invented computers and sent men to the moon met with the same sort of resistance. Computers? They were too bulky and too unwieldy. Why would anyone ever need one in their life? These innovators were willing to risk scorn and even possible failure in the hope of advancing technology and making life better for those around them.

Too many people have had their imaginations stolen by past experience. They have heard voices of derision and doubt saying such things as "You can't do that" or "That will never work; it doesn't make sense." They have reacted to these voices by giving up their quest. Too many people have lacked confidence in themselves, often because their parents failed to realize the importance of building self-esteem.

I have a close friend and prayer partner who constantly struggles with issues of self-worth. He grew up in a home where he was constantly picked on by his parents. He heard the phrase "You'll never amount to anything" so many times he began to accept it as gospel. My friend had his dreams stolen in childhood. He's now in his forties, and although he's a good Christian and a solid citizen, memories of all those discouraging words haunt him.

My friend's parents lacked the imagination to see what an outstanding person their son could become.

An Imaginative Coach

Buddy Ryan was the most imaginative guy I met in football. He dreamed up the "46" defense, which the '85 Chicago

Bears used as the basis for our Super Bowl championship. Like a real leader, Buddy asked for input from others involved in the scheme—players such as Dan Hampton, Gary Fencik, Dave Duerson, Leslie Frazier, Otis Wilson, and me. We helped him revise and refine the 46 concept.

In the 46 defense, at times I'd drop off from my linebacking spot and defend the field like a safety. "Mike, can you get underneath the receiver?" Buddy would say.

"Yes, sir," I'd reply.

"Hamp, can you hit the gap so hard you tie up two offensive lineman?" Buddy would ask, and Dan would nod that he could. "Good, because that will free up Wilber Marshall."

Fencik and Buddy worked out a deal where Gary would cheat over to the weak side, just enough to bait the opposing quarterback. Then at the snap of the ball, Fencik would start racing back over to the strong side and get a pick (interception).

Buddy kept asking for our ideas and we kept working with him. We began to feel empowered. More importantly, we had ownership in the process. We believed we could do anything we had to with the 46 if we were coordinated and trusted each other.

Some pseudo-leaders you meet in business never solicit additional opinions that might differ from their own. They are more likely to say "do it my way" than "tell me what you think about this." That kind of arrogance and misuse of their position (a common modus operandi in many businesses I've studied) does not constitute real leadership. It's autocracy.

As a leader, Buddy Ryan was criticized for his imagination. I remember that my first two years in the league Tommy Kramer and Ahmad Rashad of the Minnesota Vikings, two of the star players for our most bitter NFC Central Division rival, kept insisting the 46 defense wouldn't work. I remember Kramer being quoted as saying that the 46 defense looked like a circus. I wonder if Tommy and Ahmad thought soccer-style field goal kickers would never catch on, either.

As a leader, Buddy Ryan was prepared to fail. He knew he would have to experiment with the 46 defense before he ironed out its weaknesses. He knew he'd have to plug in the right personnel to make the defense work.

He'd invented the defense in the late 1970s, when the Bears were short on linebackers and had to flood the field with defensive backs. A few years later, after some savvy drafts and shrewd moves by the Bears front office (especially by Jim Finks and Bill Tobin), Buddy had the athletes he needed in place. When that day arrived, Buddy's 46 defense produced a world championship in Chicago and later set records in Philadelphia. Like many leaders with imagination, Buddy Ryan had the last word.

Putting Imagination to Work

I've worked out a formula to show how imagination contributes to the success of any leader. The formula goes like this:

Imagination + Persistence + Execution = Leadership

You can apply this formula to families, as well as teams.

Let me explain what I mean in family terms. For starters, Kim and I have to use imagination to project into the future and visualize what our children can become. For our kids to develop, grow, and become wholesome and whole—leaders of tomorrow—we have to be aware of the impact of things we say today.

If we were to tell our children harmful things such as "You're dumb" or "You're stupid" or "Why did I even have you? You're worthless!" it's easy to see the potential for serious damage. So Kim and I stress to our children, even when they make careless or silly mistakes, "No matter what you do,

I still love *you*. Nothing you can do will make me stop loving you. I don't care what it is, I'm going to love *you*."

I know I probably wouldn't be able to make those kinds of affirming statements without using my imagination and looking ahead. If I am doing my part as a father and co-leader in my home, however, and serving as a tool for the Lord and allowing him to work through me, such reassurance to my children comes easily. It's natural and unforced.

Persistence refers to never giving up on our kids, the way God never gives up on us. I try to relate to my children how God has dealt with my many failures and boneheaded decisions. He never gave up. He was persistent with me when I was a liar and a hypocrite, a man falling flat on his face.

Regardless of how often I screwed up, God never abandoned me. No matter how many times I came to him in prayer, pledging to change my ways (and then breaking those promises almost immediately), he persisted.

Imagination allows us to see what can be. *Persistence* keeps us striving to attain our goals. *Execution* is an extension of the two. It occurs when we respond to the Holy Spirit and allow the Lord to work with us in blessing our wives and children. Execution is finishing the job we've started. It represents follow-through.

Accountability

Real leaders don't have freedom and autonomy to run wild. They surround themselves with trusted advisers, men and women who are able to rein them in when they go off on a tangent.

We've all known individuals who reach a leadership position and suddenly, inexplicably, get caught up in the power and status that comes with the position. These people become so full of themselves that at times you're tempted to ask,

"Excuse me, who died and made you God?" To reach them on the telephone, just dial 1-800-NO-IT-ALL.

These people stop seeking new ideas. They don't want to hear the truth, they want to be reminded of their own "brilliance." They don't want anyone telling them their ideas aren't great ones. They take on a "don't confuse me with the facts" approach.

That dynamic, unfortunately, exists in many families as well. Instead of being a leader wise enough to listen and learn, dad acts as if he holds the patent to every good idea. He doesn't want to hear alternatives from his wife or children. He becomes a "my way or the highway" kind of narrow thinker.

Real leaders, by contrast, are always willing to listen to skeptics or naysayers and discern the truth from their words. Real leaders seek the counsel of people who don't sugarcoat things but give them their medicine straight. They don't keep toadies or yes-men on the payroll; they keep independent voices who will tell the truth, not what the leaders necessarily want to hear. That kind of honest criticism and contradiction gives validity to their ideas.

I learned about accountability during my days with the Chicago Bears. In our championship season, we had a perfect balance between a strong, outspoken head coach (Mike Ditka) and an equally strong and outspoken defensive coordinator (Buddy Ryan). They served, intentionally or not, as accountability partners for each other, ever ready to rein in the other.

I'm fortunate to have several accountability partners, people who keep me sharp and alert and vigilant to move forward. People who, when I ask them for an opinion, respond with the unvarnished truth. People who will tell me, plainly, when my thinking or actions are totally off-base.

One is Kim, who keeps me accountable to my family and friends. Another is my mother, who keeps me accountable to Kim. Others are Al Harris, Leslie Frazier, and Dan Rains, a trio of my former Bears teammates, who keep me accountable to my family.

I can't tell you how many times I've heard from Al, Leslie, or Dan, "Samurai [my nickname from the Bears] are you traveling too much?" or "Samurai, I don't think that's such a good idea."

These guys give me the straight skinny. They'll let me know when I've been derelict in my duties or haven't given my best or if I'm letting some family member down.

I also have an accountability partner in Rick DeMarco, an executive with Carrier Corporation. Rick and I frequently discuss leadership issues in the family and in business. He has a great grasp of management skills and is a really sharp guy.

My children also serve as accountability partners. It wasn't easy, but I learned the value of asking the kids about what kind of job I'm doing as a dad. Before I did that, though, I had to be sure that my relationship with my kids was such that they feel they can confide in me without sanction.

I challenge my kids to tell me the truth about my parenting, because that gives me the opportunity to help us both. I don't want to be left in the dark trying to help my children be the best they can be. I'll ask them, "What can daddy do to help you discover your talents and gifts? What can I do to have you understand how much I love you? How can I better show you my love? Do you have any ideas for dad that will make me a better parent? A better leader for this family? Do you have any thoughts when it comes to your siblings; do you think they feel daddy's love? Or do you feel they are being overlooked? Tell me what you see."

These kinds of accountability sessions produce plenty of useful information for how I relate to my children and how they relate to me.

Of course, the ultimate accountability partner we have for our lives is Jesus Christ. One question I constantly have to ask

God is: Am I compromising, rationalizing, or justifying what I know in my heart isn't right?

Empowerment

Leaders involve everyone in the decision-making process. They seek suggestions and comments left and right. They give family members, employees, teammates—virtually everyone involved in a decision—a say-so. By doing so, they are giving ownership.

Leaders also solicit, rather than suppress, other voices and other opinions. Why? Because great leaders are great listeners.

One of the best examples I know of someone who empowers others is Bill Pollard, the former CEO of ServiceMaster Corporation. Bill, an energetic man with a keen and penetrating mind, conducts some of the management training seminars for ServiceMaster's staff.

Talk about working a room! He will begin a seminar session by firing off questions at a rapid pace. He'll say "What do you think about this approach? Will this idea work? Will that one? Why? Why not? Tell me."

Bill Pollard stimulates conversation and forces his audience to confront key issues affecting the company's business. He has everyone in the room up on their toes and hunched forward in their seats. It's impressive to witness.

He's given me insights to apply to parenting: Always ask your children what they think about an issue. Also, always ask for a response. A shrug of their shoulders or shake of the head is not a sufficient reply. Draw them out.

Empowering our children, or giving them ownership in a decision, encourages them to think for themselves, express themselves, and make their own decisions.

I remember an incident that happened last summer. Kristen, when addressed, kept saying "yes" and "no" to one of our friends. I got on her about it that evening.

"Look, sweetheart, how many times have I told you and your brother and sisters that I want you to say 'yes sir' and 'no sir' to adults?"

"Dad, I don't understand why," she said. "If I say yes or no, that's not being disrespectful. No one I know says 'yes sir' and 'no sir.'"

"Well, you're going to say it," I countered. "Do you understand me? End of conversation."

As she walked away to go to her room, I thought to myself, I've finally got her straightened out on this. But the more I began to reflect, I realized I had once again pulled rank. To enforce his rules, Daddy had made another power play.

I called her back to the den. "Kristen, I want to walk through something with you," I said. "Now, when I'm done, the decision is going to be yours. But I want you to know that the reason I want you to say 'sir' and 'ma'am' is that people you meet have all kinds of problems and situations. You'll be amazed how often, when you use those terms of respect, people will light up. What you are saying with 'sir' and 'ma'am' shows a level of respect people don't receive much anymore. If you use those words, sweetheart, you'll find you just might make someone's day.

"It's an old habit with me. Something I grew up with, something I always do," I said. "But I'm not going to shove it down your throat. It's your option."

Kristen thought that over for a moment. "Daddy, you know what," she said, "now that you explain it, what you're saying makes sense. I would like to brighten someone's day, so I'll starting saying 'sir' and 'ma'am.'"

"Well, honey, it's up to you," I smiled.

That, to me, is an example of empowering Kristen and giving her ownership. She made the decision for herself.

Accessibility

Leaders have the ability to energize and inspire others through a direct approach. They are able to motivate, in part, because of their accessibility.

I remember that when Mike Ditka became coach of the Bears he instituted an open-door policy. He wanted to see his players and hear from them. He didn't want to erect any barriers between himself and the team. The year he took over as coach he put a one-word sign on the desk in his office. The sign, written in big block letters, read: COMMUNICATE.

Later on, Ditka would have problems with some of his players.

By then he had lost his accountability partner (Buddy Ryan) and he became more remote and distant from the team. During the NFL strike of 1987, he criticized the players for being greedy, creating a rift on the team. One of Ditka's greatest strengths as a leader—being accessible and a good "people person"—had been compromised. The level of trust players had in him was diminished and soon after the team became fragmented.

I knew Coach Ditka was frustrated. I knew he felt we had a team in 1987 that could return to the Super Bowl. Instead, the season came apart because of a strike that accomplished very little. I have wished many times since that someone could have gone to Ditka and said, "Hey, I know you're frustrated and angry, but let's look at the big picture. You've got to keep this team together."

Accessibility is a big issue with me. I spent too much time early in our marriage making myself inaccessible to Kim and the kids. I had my head buried in the Bears' playbook.

Fortunately, in the final few years of my career I refocused my vision from the Xs and Os to my wife and children.

Visibility

I believe that being accessible when someone needs to see you isn't enough. Leaders can't sit back and wait for others to come to them. They have to be out on the front line with their troops, shaking hands, asking about family members, and sharing a joke or story. They need to mix and mingle.

For example, I've read about one chief executive officer, Herb Kelleher of Southwest Airlines, who spends one working day a month performing the same tasks as his employees. One month he may be handling baggage, the next month at the ticket counter, the next refueling the jets. That's terrific leadership. He's down on the front line, with the troops, letting it all hang out. That's the stuff of truly inspiring leadership.

If dads are going to be leaders for their children, they have to be on the front line, in full view. When I'm not on the road for business reasons, you'll find me driving kids to afternoon soccer practice or attending PTA meetings at night. Whatever the activity the kids have going on, I'll be there. Count on it.

Overcome Adversity

Leaders have a mature presence in the face of adversity. They aren't Chicken Littles who think the sky is falling. They don't panic, or overreact, when things don't go as planned.

Leaders won't call out the lifeboats at the first sign of choppy water or reach for a parachute if they encounter air turbulence. Leaders are cool in the clutch, not panic-prone.

I remember when Bill Walsh and Joe Montana were starting out in San Francisco. Their first year together, the 49ers were something like 2–14, which by any definition qualifies as real adversity. Did they panic? Did they say this West Coast offense isn't going to work, let's try something else? No. They kept working at it, refining it, building on it.

Walsh stood shoulder to shoulder with Montana during the hard times. This is my guy, Walsh told anyone who would listen, this is the guy who'll get the job done. And did he ever! Joe Montana went on to become probably the best big-game quarterback in NFL history. Walsh, meanwhile, was subsequently hailed as pro football's resident genius.

It's important to remember, however, that success wasn't automatic or overnight for Walsh and Montana. Or for Pittsburgh coach Chuck Noll and his quarterback, Terry Bradshaw, during the Steelers' great run in the 1970s. They overcame adversity. They worked through the tough times. They persevered.

Our Greatest Trial

Kim and I have been blessed with six great children, but we faced one painful period in 1990 when we lost a child during the fifth month of her pregnancy.

I'll never forget the day at Bears training camp in Platteville, Wisconsin, when Coach Ditka called me over. "Mike, you've got to go home," he said. "Kim needs you there. There's something wrong with the baby. Sounds serious, son. Good luck."

Chills came over me. I started shaking. I immediately left camp and flew home, worrying the whole time about Kim and wondering what had happened. I kept saying to the Lord, "Why us?"

When I reached Chicago, I learned that the baby's umbilical cord had knotted around his ankle and he (a boy) hadn't been able to receive any nourishment from Kim. Doctors didn't discover the problem until it was too late to save his life.

Kim had to deliver the dead infant. I'll never forget the pain and heartache in her face when she came out of the delivery room. We held each other tightly and wouldn't let go. Without question, that was the saddest time of our life together.

I stayed home for several days, during which time Kim and I tried to be strong for each other. Then I returned to training camp and she went back to being a full-time mom. We already had three little ones running around the house.

We never completely came to terms with our grief until about two years ago. During a vacation to Grand Cayman, Kim and I started bickering and arguing over a bunch of petty, nit-picking things. Suddenly, I felt the presence of the evil one in our hotel room, doing his best to come between us.

I commanded that evil presence to leave us alone. "In the holy name of Jesus Christ," I said, "get out of this room. Leave now."

Kim and I walked over to the bed and sat down.

"Sweetheart, what's wrong?" I said in my most tender voice. "Please tell me."

"I'm mad, Mike," she sobbed. "I'm angry with God for allowing our little boy to die. I felt he could have done something to save our child. Why didn't he?"

Between our tears, we talked about our tragic loss and how only God knows why such things happen. Up to that point, Kim had had uneventful pregnancies where everything went smoothly. We had assumed they'd all be that way. "One day we'll see the Lord in glory and ask him why he needed our baby in heaven," I said.

Kim and I made it through that agonizing episode and were strengthened by it. As leaders, we didn't let it ruin our family. We didn't overreact and stop having children. We didn't seek refuge in alcohol or drugs or other crutches. We didn't turn away from each other, as many dads and moms do after tragedy strikes their family.

Over the course of time, Kim and I have dealt with the pain. We finally felt closure last year when we named the infant Cody. That's the name we had picked out back in 1990.

We shared our pain with the children and let them know our faith is very real. They saw firsthand that you can feel hurt with God, even question him, but ultimately trust him with all that you have. We placed our trust in the Lord and kept leading our family, which has swelled from three to six children since we lost our second son.

CHAPTER 9

Caring Through Communication

There is a social services organization in Dallas—The Child Care Group*—that has earned national acclaim for its pioneering programs in the areas of child care and child development.

Over the past two decades, the organization has developed and refined an innovative program called Relationship-Centered Child Care®. As its name suggests, Relationship-Centered Child Care is based on developing and maintaining close relationships between infants, toddlers, preschoolers, their parents, and primary caregivers.

Adding an important dimension to this unique program is the family grouping of youngsters (generally from low-income, single-parent homes) into groups of five for children under three (with only two babies under eighteen months) and groups of nine for children ages three to five. In effect, the Child Care Group creates family models.

Sonya Bemporad, an expert in early childhood development and one of the driving forces behind Relationship-Centered Child Care, explains that family grouping allows

---

*The Child Care Group, which operates child development centers and family day homes in Dallas, has been an industry leader in designing child care programs for U.S. corporations. Information about its innovative programs is available at 214–630–7911.

children and their caregivers to remain together over a period of years.

These extended relationships provide the emotional investment, attachment, and growth in early childhood that enables babies to mature into moral and ethical young adults. In addition, the constancy of these relationships gives youngsters a sense of security and well-being and helps with socialization skills. They learn how to play and interact with others.

A "white paper" on Relationship-Centered Child Care prepared by Sonya Bemporad and Roberta Bergman of The Child Care Group makes the point that babies cannot thrive in environments in which relationships are transitory: "At best, they will emerge with diminished capacity for learning and normal relationships. At worst, the children will grow up without the capacity for conscience, without the capacity to learn and without the capacity for empathy—the qualities that make us human."

The Child Care Group's approach gives youngsters a head-start in life. Children who have received child care administered by the organization outperform their peers on standardized achievement testing and are less likely to have to repeat a grade. Their futures are brightened immeasurably by their early-life experience.

What Does This Mean for Dad?

The implications of The Child Care Group's breakthrough work in basing child development on relationships and bonding should be obvious to fathers. Dad, not just mom, must serve as a primary caregiver in the home. His relationship with children, from the earliest moments of infancy, is just as critical as hers.

In recent years, many fathers have become more involved in childbirth (beyond their biological role in procreation). Instead of pacing around the waiting room, handing out cigars, dad is likely to be in the delivery room, helping mom with her breathing, mopping her brow, and giving encouragement. While that's commendable, daddy's role doesn't begin and end with Lamaze classes, or putting on a hospital gown and using a videocamera to document baby's birth; when the infant emerges from the womb, dad's job is just beginning.

From the outset, dads need to cradle babies in their arms and press them to their chest, allowing the infant to feel their heart beat, touch their face, pull on their ears, smell them. Dads have to learn to hold their babies adeptly, not awkwardly. (Some fathers I've seen hold their infants as though they're handling nitroglycerin or TNT.)

Daddy needs to coo and whisper—just like mommy—words of reassurance and praise. He needs to sing his share of lullabies.

The reason, say Bemporad and Bergman of The Child Care Group, is that "For a baby to develop a sense of the importance of close relationships, he or she must experience them. A baby must learn to love. He or she must differentiate *this* face and *this* voice from other faces and voices so that this particular relationship can be appreciated."

An infant's ability to make these kind of associations begins in his or her first few months. Dad can't be missing from the equation, waiting for the baby to walk and talk or throw and catch a ball, before he becomes a father. He has to begin creating his own relationship with his child—the sooner the better.

Cracking the Rock

Many fathers, unless they are rooting for their favorite football team to punch the ball into the end zone or perhaps watching a veterans' parade on Memorial Day or the Fourth of July, tend to keep their emotions in check. When it comes to men, our culture has traditionally equated silence with strength and tenderness with weakness.

Some dads I know do a great job of communicating. The relationships they establish with their children are honest, open, and interactive. They get along like best pals.

But many men are distant and detached. They have been conditioned to let down their guard as often as Mike Tyson, George Foreman, or Evander Holyfield. As a result, some children have had to grow up with fathers who exude the warmth and emotional texture of the Rock of Gibraltar.

We all know grown men and women who still suffer because of daddy's inability to communicate with them during their formative years. These adults have an empty space inside that's difficult to fill, largely because they interpreted the silent treatment from daddy as a form of rejection.

Although some men are more introverted than others, all dads should recognize how vital communicating and nurturing is to a child's healthy development.

Real Men Cry

Our family attended a special pageant of Christmas music at our church during the holidays last year. The combination of the familiar hymns and carols and the rich voices of the Willow Creek choir stirred my spirit. Tears streamed out of my eyes and ran down my cheeks.

I suddenly felt a tug on my hand. It was Matthew.

"Is something wrong, Dad?" he asked.

"No, son," I blubbered. "I'm just happy that we have a loving God who cares for us. And I'm happy we have a family that loves each other so much."

I want our children to know how much I treasure their being. I'm not ashamed to let them see me cry tears of joy. By being open and vulnerable in their presence, I'm demonstrating that they can come to me without any reservations, bringing their fears and worries. They know my concern is genuine and heartfelt.

I can't believe any parents would bring children into this world intending to neglect them, or abandon them. Parents have every good intention when our kids are born. Somehow, though, many of us fathers have allowed other things—like jobs and careers—to create walls between our children and ourselves.

Listen Up

Constant communication between parents and children develops family bonds and wards off feelings of isolation and distrust. How many times have we read about disaffected youth who have turned to gang membership or drugs because they felt unwelcome or unloved at home?

I've met many kids who tell me the main thing that's missing at home is communication with their parents. They want someone to hear them out. They want someone willing to *listen* to them.

Daddy needs to talk to his children, at length, every day. If he's away from home on a business trip, he should call each night and talk to each child individually. If that's not possible, write a note or letter to let them know how much you care.

If dad never allows a day to pass without communicating with children, they will feel valued. His words will have a profound effect on raising their self-esteem.

A Note to Kristen

I was on a business trip a couple years ago and decided to call home to talk to our children before they left for school. I spoke with all the kids except Kristen, who was still in the shower. "Tell her I'll call back in a few minutes," I told Kim.

On that particular day, Kristen had a big test at school. I wanted her to know I was praying for her and that I love her.

Before I could call back, however, the executives I was meeting came to my hotel room and we began working. By the time we finished, the school day had already begun. So I called Kristen's school and reached the nurse. I asked her to take this message: "Kristen, I'm sorry I missed speaking with you this morning. I just wanted to wish you good luck on today's test. I know you'll do your best. Most of all, I want you to know how special you are and how much I love you."

Kristen was so proud of that note from her daddy she kept it on her desk for the rest of the school year.

Kids Say the Darndest Things

If you listen closely to your children, you'll see how bright, imaginative, and amazing they really are. Of course, sometimes they'll throw you for a complete loop.

I was sitting in the family room one day last year, watching the children play, when I noticed Jackie getting more and more perturbed.

"It's my turn. It's my turn!" she shouted at her sister.

I couldn't imagine what the commotion was about. "What's wrong, Jackie?"

"Brooke won't let me play with the airplane," she blurted out. "It's my turn. I want to play with the airplane, too."

"Airplane? I don't see any airplane. What are you talking about?"

Jackie pointed at Brooke, who had cupped her wrist and was moving her hand around to simulate an airplane coming in for landing. It was a make-believe plane.

"Are you kidding me?" I laughed. "Now I have to referee a dispute over an imaginary airplane? I don't believe it."

I talked Brooke into allowing Jackie to fly the airplane.

Sharing toys—real or imagined—is always a good lesson for children to learn.

Reading Aloud Together

I believe one of the best ways parents and children can communicate is by reading aloud with each other. Regardless of whether the material is Dr. Seuss, the "Spot" series, Precious Moments, or the illustrated Bible, reading aloud together serves as a way for dads and moms to convey thoughts and ideas and teach moral lessons, a way they can communicate their values and beliefs.

Parents can also use books when they are uncertain how to discuss a difficult subject. Bookstores and libraries are filled with good children's books that deal with such topics as a family move, arguments with friends, poor performance in schools, or the death of a loved one.

The communication that occurs when we read aloud with our children isn't just one-way, though. While our kids can learn from the experience, so can we. Children often find it easier to let us in on what they are feeling—including what's puzzling or troubling them—if they can do so in the context of a book or story. Reading about the experiences (good and bad) of others teaches our children that they are not the only ones to encounter such things. That knowledge can be reassuring. It can also serve to encourage our children to talk to us about what's going on in their lives.

One of my co-author's favorite, most vivid childhood memories is of his mother tucking him into bed at night and reading to him from *One Hundred and One Famous Poems*. As he grew older, the ritual changed and he began reading the poems aloud to her ("The Highwayman" by Alfred Noyes was a particular favorite).

Not only did those moments of reading together deepen the bond between mother and son, the steady exposure to the richness and breadth of the English language led him to a career as a professional writer.

Rewards of Reading

By encouraging children to read, and reading aloud with them, parents give children a tremendous advantage. Research has shown that children who acquire reading skills early have a jump-start on life. These children consistently outperform kids whose reading skills lag behind.

It's also been documented that children who read well are more likely to complete high school, enter college, complete college, perhaps do post-graduate work. Their career opportunities broaden, they increase their earning power, they are more likely to achieve success in their chosen field.

Children who read well develop skills for critical thinking and analysis. They learn to appreciate opinions and points of view. They learn that experiences in life aren't always black or white, but some gradation on the color scale. Readers learn to think independently, not just go along with the crowd.

I think one of the best things we can do as dads is to get our children engaged in a reading program. Reading is a valuable exercise because it leads to knowledge and—as the saying goes—knowledge is power.

One of the principal ways we acquire and assimilate knowledge is through reading history, literature, and science, and reading about individuals who won battles, led expeditions, discovered cures for disease, created great works of art, and walked on the moon—people who made a difference.

Famous people have always fascinated me. As a youngster, I read biographies about people such as Abraham Lincoln and George Washington Carver, people who had a huge impact on the American way of life. Years later, I'm still reading as much as possible.

I encourage dads to pull their heads out of the sports page or their briefcases and start reading aloud with their children. Revisit some of the favorite books of your own youth, whether they be Jack London's adventures or the Leatherstocking tales or the Hardy Boys. By sharing the magic of those experiences, you will be enriching them. Even just ten minutes a day together can form a father-child bond.

Conversations with My Mom

Probably an even more important communication tool than reading aloud together, though, is simply talking with your children. In other words, giving them your time and undivided attention.

During my teenage years at home, after my father had left the family and my older brothers and sisters had moved out, my mother and I would talk for hour upon hour each evening. Those conversations meant more to me—then and now—than any cartoon show or sitcom or cop show or football game I could have been watching on TV. They were a primary part of my education about life.

My mother would listen to whatever was bothering me. She'd patiently answer my questions about everything from A to Z. Oh, she'd correct my grammar now and again and try to help me eliminate slang I'd picked up in the neighborhood, but she heard me out. She listened with both her ears and her heart. She helped me learn to organize my thoughts and express them and by doing so, gave me the foundation on which to build my career as a public speaker.

I didn't do all the talking, of course. My mother would tell me stories about her upbringing, about her courtship with my dad, about my brothers and sisters, all of whom are considerably older than I am. She would explain some of the decisions they had made in their lives, point out some mistakes they might have been able to correct. She didn't want me to repeat those same mistakes.

My mother had several themes she liked to reinforce: Stand up for your beliefs; always tell the truth; be real—don't try to be something or someone you are not; be careful where you go and what you do, what you eat and what you drink; if a situation looks murky or potentially dangerous, get the heck out of there; don't hang around waiting for trouble to break out, because it probably will.

My mother stressed that people should try to live by the Golden Rule. "Michael," she said, "the only way you're going to make it in life is to treat people the way you want to be treated. Be kind to them and honest with them."

I can also remember her saying, "When a person tries to live a godly life, to stand up for himself and do what is right, he will not be liked. You might as well be prepared for that."

"Being a Christian takes courage," she told me. "It means making a commitment to doing the right thing, not necessarily the thing that will be popular. It means going against the grain at times, having the personal strength not to conform for the sake of conformity. When you're a Christian, you will have to walk alone at times, but with God in your life you will never be lonely."

My mother also taught me that being a Christian means standing up for the underdogs and outcasts in life. In high school, for example, I can recall several times talking down bullies who were picking on some of the smaller and weaker guys in the class.

One time, on a field trip for our drafting class, two bullies decided to take the T-square and protractor of one of the meek little guys.

"Those are his," I told them. "Give them back. Don't treat him that way."

"Who's going to make us?" asked one of the bullies.

"I am," I said calmly, though to be honest I was getting ready to go to the mat. "If you're picking on him, you're picking on me. Are you *sure* you want to do that?"

The bullies thought better of going to fist city with me and gave my classmate back his drafting materials. I'm glad we didn't come to blows, because fighting should be a last resort. No one ever wins in a fight.

My courage, as well as a sense of duty to protect others, was tested again when two white kids, a brother and sister, transferred into all-black Attucks Junior High. Many students, including some of my own friends, treated them with scorn. I found out that racism and bigotry don't travel down a one-way street.

I befriended the two white kids and ate with them in the school cafeteria. I tried to put the Golden Rule into practice. I did my best to protect the kids from the taunts and racial epithets my African-American schoolmates were dishing out. Finally, though, the kids had enough abuse and transferred to a different school district.

More Motherly Advice

My mother also talked to me about girls, how to choose a steady date and what qualities to look for in a prospective mate. She told me to make sure that any girl I was starting to get serious about showed respect for herself, as well as for others. My mother told me to look for a girl with goals and ambition, someone determined to make the most of her life.

Mom cautioned me to avoid the kind of girls who use sex as a bargaining tool. "You be careful, Michael," she'd say. "You don't want to wind up being one of those young men who becomes a father and doesn't even know if the baby is his."

She didn't really have to tell me to avoid "fast" girls. I was aware enough to know that teenage girls who behave in such a manner have no respect for themselves.

I can never fully express my appreciation for those lessons my mother taught me. I can't think of a better education a boy can receive—unless it's from his mom *and* dad. Children can learn so much from their parents (and grandparents), if dad and mom are willing to open up and communicate.

My mother, through our nightly conversations, was expressing her parental love. She was helping me sort out all the problems and difficulties teenagers experience. She was helping me focus on the possibilities in life. Through her warmth and reassurance, she was trying her best to fill my spirit with goodness.

Sure, I made mistakes. Sure, I entertained some impure thoughts. Sure, I was tempted to do the wrong thing. What teenage boy or girl hasn't been?

Mom's love provided me with structure and guidelines. She calmed the waters that churned inside my soul. She pointed me in a direction of service. What we shared, after my sister Rudell moved out, was family time. I deeply regretted that my daddy wasn't home to share his stories and insights, but even so, those conversations were the most meaningful moments in my young life.

My mother also taught me about choosing friends carefully. She cautioned me about falling in with the wrong crowd at school, or in the neighborhood. Even though she was busy working day and night, she kept tabs on my whereabouts so she could account for my time. When I went over to visit my best friend, Ron Williams, she knew what we were doing. We established curfews, so I wasn't out running in the streets after hours. This form of discipline demonstrated her love for me, and I accepted it willingly. Okay, maybe ninety-five percent willingly. We had our disagreements.

She also warned me about the dangers of using drugs. Not that my eyes were closed and my mind was shut about the matter. If you looked around the neighborhood, you couldn't help but see people tossing away their present and future, shooting heroin or smoking marijuana, blaming their troubles on "the system." These people were waiting for a break in life, instead of going out and making their own breaks. They had surrendered without putting up a fight to solve their problems. They had totally copped out.

Ultimately, family time with my mother meant more to the development of young Mike Singletary than all those Friday nights I strapped on a helmet and pads for the Worthing Colts and started busting heads and making plays all over the field.

Football was my gift from God, the talent he gave me to push to the limit, but my essence isn't about being a head-hunter, the baddest man to back up the line of scrimmage. My essence revolves around the kind of man I become. To be the husband and father I want to be, I must keep the channels of communication open in our family at all times, the way my mother did. I have to be listening to my wife and kids—and then responding.

A Lesson to Remember

A lesson my mother stressed to me, one that Kim and I try to communicate to our kids, is that children shouldn't feel they always have to go along with the crowd. In other words, they should dare to be different.

It's conforming to the dictates and desires of others, not following personal convictions, that gets many kids today in trouble. Many children lack the value system, or enough belief in themselves, to withstand temptation.

I was talking to our children at the dinner table one night about the various roads we can choose to travel in life. Some of them are straight and narrow, others are winding and crooked and lead goodness-knows-where.

I drew a picture to illustrate the point. "Say, for example, this is the interstate we're traveling on," I said, drawing a white line down the middle to separate the road into two lanes.

In the right lane, I wrote the words "wants to be admired; wants to be accepted; wants to be liked." In the left lane I wrote the words "character, convictions, leadership."

Then I asked our kids to name some of their heroes. The names Michael Jordan, Kristi Yamaguchi, and Tiger Woods came up immediately. One of the kids, eager to please Dad, said Mike Singletary.

"When you think about these people, which lane of the interstate do you think they traveled down?" I asked.

"The left one?"

"That's right. When their friends encouraged them to take a drink or have a smoke, do you think they went along with it because they wanted to be liked or admired?

"Or do you suppose they held to their convictions and kept practicing their basketball and figure skating?"

The kids agreed that these athletes had not been swayed by temptation to follow the crowd but had remained true to their chosen path. They knew which side of the road they wanted to travel.

"All you see on the TV screen is the finished product," I said. "If Michael Jordan dunks the ball, or Kristi Yamaguchi makes a spinning jump, or Tiger Woods hits the golf ball close to the pin, you are fascinated by how they make it look so easy. What you don't see is the effort it took for them to reach that level. And you don't see their determination to choose a road and follow it, steering clear of distractions. *That's* what makes them champions. The fact they've remained true to themselves."

I have those kinds of conversations with my children all the time. By communicating constantly, by telling them stories and sharing the wisdom I've acquired, I am demonstrating how much I care. The security children gain from knowing that daddy and mommy love them totally helps them fulfill their potential and become whatever they dream to be.

Shared Wisdom

One of the best decisions Kim and I have made as a couple was to invite her grandparents to live with us for several years. We had an apartment built for them on the second floor of our home, over our garage. Even though the kitchen downstairs was nearly as large as their whole apartment, our family would gravitate each morning to Nana and Papa's kitchen upstairs.

Our children knew they could always go to Nana and Papa for hugs and kisses and unlimited lap time. They were always available for storytelling and playing games.

It's my opinion that wisdom shared by older people—especially grandparents and others who love you—is invaluable to a person's growth and development.

CHAPTER 10

Make the Most of Family Time

As I learned from those conversations with my mother, family time is invaluable. It's worth more than all the gold in Fort Knox.

Family time represents the most important waking hours we spend on this earth. Daddy needs to recognize and understand that fact and plan his daily activities accordingly.

In the Singletary household, we make a conscious effort to maximize family time in the evening. We eat our dinner together, all eight of us, and we don't get up and dash toward the television when the meal is done. We sit around and *communicate*. Our conversation centers on what happened at school that day or what family projects are coming up.

We play games together. We joke, laugh, and act silly. Some people probably think I'm the most serious-minded person they've ever met, but around my wife and children I can be a real clown. I may not challenge Sinbad or Jim Carrey on the laugh-o-meter, but I do have a good sense of humor. All my children think I'm hilarious. But when I start cutting up, Kim gets up from the table and starts washing the dishes, so maybe I'm not as funny as I think I am.

Sometimes Kim and I use family time to teach our children lessons about life. For example, we might give the kids an assignment like putting together a program on courage.

A few nights later, the children will perform a skit or act out famous moments in history, and then the whole family will discuss what courage means and how it's demonstrated.

Sometimes, we do role-playing at the dinner table. We'll create a scenario and act it out, swapping roles. One of the children will play the role of Kim, another will play my part. Kim and I will pretend to be one of the children.

This role-playing can be revealing. Not only do we learn more about ourselves, it's always good for plenty of laughter. Kim and I gain incredible insight into how our children perceive us, and we find out if our teaching and communication skills are effective.

Some evenings, we might play a game like "going to the store." One of the kids will play the part of a merchant; the other kids will be shoppers. We pretend we're looking for specific items and we act out a scenario where sales take place.

What we're attempting to do is teach our kids lessons about life. Lessons like how to treat customers and respond to their needs. What inventory is. How to close a sale. The children who play the shoppers learn how to inspect merchandise and tell about quality. How to know when they're getting a good deal. What credit cards are all about. What the term "lay-away" means.

That's just one example. What these scenarios accomplish, besides providing interaction with dad and mom, is to teach our children something useful that they can apply in their own lives. Something more meaningful than they'd learn playing a video game.

A Favorite Story

Sometimes Kim and I will tell the kids stories from our past, when we were their age. They never get tired of hearing about the time my mother took me to buy a new pair of shoes.

Naturally, I hated the shoes she had picked out for me. They looked too boxy for my taste.

"Tell us that story again, Daddy, the one about the shoes," the kids beg. And I will, adopting the voice and manner of my mother, acting out that long-ago scene in a Montgomery Ward store.

"Mama, I can't wear these shoes, they're too tight," I pleaded, my eyes on another pair I'd set my heart on. Cool shoes.

"Don't tell me they don't fit, young man," said Mama, sounding like Aunt Esther on *Sanford and Son,* the woman who used to vex Redd Foxx. "Now, Mister Man, you get my boy in these shoes right here."

"But mama, please, I don't like them. . . ."

"Make your mind up, Michael. Either you take this pair, which we can afford, or keep what you have on."

That pretty much sealed the deal. The shoes I was wearing had cardboard in the bottom and weren't a pretty sight. I agreed to get the ones my mother wanted. At least they were new.

The kids will erupt in laughter, especially when I do all the voices and talk silly. Like many children, my kids find it hard to believe that mommy and daddy once were little, too.

Once in a while I'll tell the children other stories from when I was growing up, stories with a moral that I hope they will apply to their own young lives.

I was no angel in high school, by any means, but I had high standards. I didn't smoke, or drink, and I didn't hang around, wasting time. Some kids in the neighborhood teased me about being a baby, a mama's boy. To be honest, that bothered me at times. But in the long run, having the high standards my mother helped me set paid off.

I know that other kids I grew up with were smarter than me and a lot more talented, but they never made it because they had no rules, no boundaries, and no direction.

Cut Off the TV

Another thing we do to maximize family time is limit television viewing. Our children don't watch TV on school nights, and on the weekends we stay so busy with organized activities, like team sports, that even Saturday morning cartoon sessions are rare.

We try to limit viewing in our family because TV programs not only are prone to be violent, but they tend to emphasize the cheap and tawdry in life. TV programs tend to be sensationalized and focused on the worst aspects of human behavior, not the best. Those aren't the kinds of lessons we want taught in our home.

To me, TV viewing can be an addiction. Like drug use, it's an escape from reality. Most popular TV drama shows these days are heavy on "realism"—cop shows, medical shows—but it's an artificial reality. The popular sitcoms these days seem to be about stressed-out yuppies trying to cope with living in the big city and trying to make connections with a small circle of friends. And the so-called family shows are centered around children who show little respect for their parents and feature parents with little respect for themselves.

That's not appropriate fare for young minds. Not when our children can be acquiring useful information or spending time bonding with their sisters and brothers.

Although I try to keep up with the Chicago Bears, I watch very little football on TV and hardly any sports shows. Not because I'm trying to distance myself from my past—I'm proud of my career—but because sports on television can take a big bite out of your free time. If I'm going to watch a ball game, it will be one of my kids' soccer games. Live and in-person.

Make Family Time Fun

Kim often reminds me that we have to make family time fun. It can't all be serious. Families need to play together and laugh together and learn to compete together in a healthy way.

I probably can't say enough about how important the gift of laughter is to a family. Homes should be fun, and kids need to learn that it's okay to laugh, that not everything in life has to be serious and solemn. Sometimes Kim and I will lead by example, showing the kids how we have fun in our relationship. I sit around and make jokes or act silly and the kids get a charge from that. Or we'll put on some dance music and work on the Macarena. Even the little ones join in.

Maximizing Family Time

All parents face a time crunch and have to perform a balancing act between family, careers, and other activities. Here are a few ideas on how parents and children can get the most out of their time together:

1. *Listen to each other.* No topic is too insignificant for a family to discuss. If it's something on your child's mind, air it out. Chances are that if one of your children brings up a subject, the kids have already talked about it. Give it its due. My only additional advice is to limit the time any one person can talk.
2. *Turn off the telephone.* Sorry, no interruptions during family time. When we're spending time with each other, everything else is secondary. In fact, we don't answer the telephone unless one of our kids is out of the house, which shows our children just how important they are. Just leave a message and we'll call back.
3. *Everyone participates.* We want all the kids engaged in the conversation. No one sits it out and retreats into a shell. As soon as you are old enough to talk, you have

the stage in our house. We're a family—we play together, pray together, and stay together. If one of the children is in a bad mood, we'll draw him or her out. Talking about your troubles is therapeutic, in case you didn't know. We let everything hang out.

4. *Ask questions.* We stimulate conversation. We discuss things we're doing, activities at school, or whatever. Or we'll share viewpoints and opinions about what's in the daily newspaper. What we're trying to accomplish is to know everything that's happening in each other's life. Our family doesn't have secrets.
5. *Don't get into a routine.* Kim and I are big believers in keeping family time fresh and alive and unpredictable. For example, let your children come up with the topic for discussion. Let them plan the program. Give them ownership in the family.
6. *Be creative.* Always look for new ways to teach lessons to your children. The people parents are competing with—TV and movie producers, game and toy manufacturers—are creative as all get out. Parents have to be, too.
7. *Avoid retreat centers.* Kim and I have received great advice, in many areas, from our good friends, Sparky and Merrie Beckham. Merrie suggested that we not allow our children to have a TV in their own room. This doesn't win us any popularity votes with our children, but it eliminates a retreat center.

Teenagers, in particular, go through a difficult time with communication, and a TV in their bedroom can draw them away from the family. If you have problems (and you will) get them out in the open and get them resolved.

Learning a Lesson

I remember asking the kids at the dinner table one night last year, "From which of these cups would you rather drink?"

I'd taken six cups out to the backyard and rubbed mud on the outside of three of them. In the other three cups, which were clean on the outside, I'd mixed some dirt and grass with water. I sat the cups on the table and told the kids to make a choice.

All of them picked the cups that were clean on the outside, of course. "Okay," I said, "take a sip from the cup in front of you. Everybody drink up."

Kristen raised the cup toward her lips, then noticed the murky liquid inside. "Yuck!" she exclaimed. "The water is dirty, Daddy."

"Now you've learned an important lesson about life that I want you to remember," I said. "Things aren't always as they seem on the outside. That's the same with people. They may seem perfectly clean and respectable on the outside, but on the inside they might be impure or maybe even evil.

"Don't be fooled by appearances; what's inside another human being is what matters most," I said. "I want each of you to learn to look at your friends and other people from the inside-out, not the outside-in. Judge them for their character and how they behave, not the color of their skin or the way they wear their hair. Sometimes appearance says a lot about a person—but many times you'll be misled."

When I talk about family time and how daddy needs to play a central role in it, some people think I've gone loco. They insist that males are incapable of intimate communication, even with their own kids. Men's personalities often are too rigid, too closed.

I disagree. Dads can be their kids' best pal. Dads can lower their guard and reveal their softer side, without having children lose respect for them. Dads can drop the "tough-guy" façade and, along with mom, make family time enjoyable, educational—and an everyday occurrence.

CHAPTER 11

In Defense of Discipline

Any discussion about family leadership and parental love must also include another crucial component—discipline. Parenting that blends love and discipline can produce a special child. A child destined to become a real "difference maker."

With many kids, though, parental love and discipline never quite get in sync. Some children starve for love from their parents but receive plenty of discipline. Others are showered with love and affection but get no discipline.

Somewhere along the line in the evolution of parenting, the concept of teaching children discipline and respect for others got misplaced or lost. So did the concept of administering discipline to kids through corporal punishment, or spanking.

Why discipline fell out of favor, I can't say for sure, although I suspect it may have been because many parents ran up a white flag at the effort and consistency required. As divorce rates rose and more mothers were forced to go to work to support families, many parents were just too tired, or too filled with guilt about breaking up their families, to adhere to boundaries or enforce family rules.

Lord knows, it can be a challenge to mete out discipline fairly and even-handedly. Sadly, some parents step over the boundary with spanking and become abusive to their children.

It's difficult for parents to administer discipline wisely and dispassionately unless they first have self-discipline themselves.

We probably would all like to see more disciplined behavior on display throughout society in general but particularly among children and teenagers. What we encounter instead is disrespect—for individuals, for institutions, for authority. That has to change. If the trend continues, you can forget about having a great America. We'll be mediocre at best. As a nation, we're only as strong as the respect we have for one another.

R-E-S-P-E-C-T

By discipline, I'm talking about a code of behavior or conduct. Used in that context, discipline means having and showing respect for yourself and others. Respect for friends, parents, teachers, principal, coaches, babysitters—or even total strangers. Respect for the man or woman who collects the garbage, pumps gas into your car, collects the ticket at the movie theater, hands out coupons at the grocery store, comes to fix the telephone line, or delivers the mail.

Respect entails basic forms of politeness and courtesy. As I mentioned earlier, I'm a stickler for saying "sir" and "ma'am." I was taught at an early age to address adults by "Mr." or "Mrs." I was taught to say "please" and "thank you" whenever someone extended a courtesy or did something on my behalf.

As I got older, I became aware that the use of those words and phrases carries an important message. Sure, I could mouth them by rote, but I consciously choose to say "Yes, sir" and "No, sir" because of what those phrases convey to the listener. They say, "I respect you. You are important to me. You are worthy of my respect."

You can bet that Kim and I are teaching our own children the same things. Because saying things like "yeah" or "huh?" or "Un-huh" shows no respect at all.

Making these lessons last can be difficult because of the influences kids are exposed to each day at school, on the playground, on the bus riding home. I've been to some birthday parties where kids show no respect for their parents. I've been to schools and seen the way kids talk back to their teachers. I've heard children at restaurants or in retail shops talk back to their parents or sass waiters or sales clerks.

I'm sure my own kids have been disrespectful from time to time; they're not saints.

But as part of our kids' continuing education in life, part of the molding of their characters, Kim and I will continue to stress that politeness and consideration for others is not a harmful or painful exercise. Rather, it's an expression of your best self.

Respect also entails a recognition of the fundamental worth of others. As a Christian, I believe that all human beings are worthy of respect because we are God's creations. Everyone is worthy of my esteem and respect—until they demonstrate through malice or mischief some reason for me to conclude otherwise.

The boorish behavior we encounter daily, from the driver on the freeway who cuts abruptly into our lane, to the chatterboxes at the movie who talk over the performance, to the knuckleheads who sprinkle expletives into their everyday conversation, is a reflection of this lack of fundamental respect for others. It also reflects that some people put down others to make themselves feel better.

If you're going to respect others, you must first respect yourself. The simple fact that so many people are rude or insensitive or callous demonstrates one of the primary failures of modern parenting: the failure to instill in children self-esteem and self-respect.

If a child feels good about himself or herself and has self-esteem and self-assurance, that child will project a positive attitude. If, however, a child feels lousy about himself or herself or has low self-esteem, chances are the kid will either be indifferent, rude, or maybe even hostile toward others.

With daddy often gone, or with mommy out working one or two jobs to make ends meet, many kids aren't made to feel welcome and worthy in this world. Sooner or later, you will encounter their rudeness, their lack of respect for everything and everybody.

A Super-Bowl Encounter

I remember taking my son Matt with me out to Phoenix for Super Bowl XXX, where the Dallas Cowboys beat the Pittsburgh Steelers. The league had set up a "Fan Forum" exhibition, and football fans were going around shaking hands with past and present NFL stars.

I heard a man standing several feet away tell his son, "Look, that's Mike Singletary, of the Chicago Bears." The kid, who was wearing a Troy Aikman jersey, didn't know Mike Singletary from Mike Ditka, but that was no big deal. From his vantage point, I was just another autograph to score.

The boy held out a Super Bowl XXX program and demanded "Gimme your autograph."

"What do you say," I asked him.

He shot me a bewildered look. "What do you mean?"

"Have you ever heard of saying *please*?" I asked.

"*Please* gimme your autograph," the boy said, straining to get out the first word. I signed my name and my number (50) and held out the program without letting go.

"What else are you supposed to say?" I asked him.

"Thank you," he said halfheartedly, racing off toward the imposing physical presence of another former NFL player. The boy's father just gave me a shrug, as if to say, "Kids, what can you do with them?" Teach them some manners, I wanted to say. Teach them to respect other people.

Setting Standards

Another form of discipline for children revolves around setting standards for household responsibilities and chores. Discipline is required to do little things like make the bed, pick up clothes, and put away toys. Discipline is needed to finish homework assignments before turning on the television or playing video games.

I believe in instilling this kind of discipline as soon as possible. For example, I began working with Jackie, getting her to help Mommy with the daily laundry, when she was three. I remember the first time I asked her to help. She was playing with a doll on the den floor when I interrupted her.

"Sweetheart," I said, "I want you to take this pile of dirty clothes up to the laundry room and put it in the pink basket, then come right back here. Do you think you can do that in two minutes?"

Jackie said she thought she could. She gathered up the pile of clothes in her little arms and trundled off toward the staircase.

Seconds later, she returned.

"Did you get the job done just like I asked you?" I inquired.

She shook her head up and down in the affirmative.

"You mean you went all the way up the stairs to the laundry room and back," I quizzed her, looking at my watch. She hadn't been gone for more than a few seconds. "Okay, then, let's go upstairs and have a look."

"No, Daddy, let me look first," Jackie blurted out, and raced back toward the hallway. I knew something was up. Turns out, she had left the pile of laundry on the second step.

So, this time, together, we walked up the stairs to the laundry room and put the clothes in the pink basket. "Was that so hard, honey?" I asked her. She shook her head side to side. "No, Daddy, it wasn't."

That's another important facet of parenting: follow-through. Often you may feel too tired or exhausted to see if your children have completed their chores. But it's imperative to check that they did exactly what was assigned. If they did, you're in business. If they didn't, it's time to take remedial steps.

Matt and the Garbage

On one occasion I vividly recall, Matt failed to take out the garbage after dinner. That was his responsibility and he knew it: it was a no-brainer. As events unfolded, though, he went to bed that evening saying he felt like he was coming down with a cold.

I arose early the next morning and was already on the Stair-master, working out, when I heard the sound of a garbage collection truck rumbling through the neighborhood. It had been a particularly cold January night in the Chicago area, meaning there was snow on the ground and ice on the driveway. I looked out the front window and saw that our cans, which sit out near the curb, weren't overflowing with Hefty bags.

The trash cans of the Singletary family, with six kids and two adults, not crammed to capacity or overflowing? I knew right away something was wrong. That simply didn't compute.

Sure enough, the trash bags were still inside the house, lying next to the garage door, waiting to be transported outside.

A small voice inside my head said, "Mike, let the boy sleep. He's not feeling well." A louder voice inside my head over-ruled, "Mike, taking out the trash is Matt's responsibility. He knows that. Those trash bags aren't going to crawl outside like an army of ants."

So I headed straight to his bedroom. "Matt, get up." I gently shook him. "The trash is still in the garage."

"But Daddy ..." he started, "I was gonna ..."

I quickly cut him off. "It's your responsibility, Matt. You were supposed to do the job last night. Get up, get out there and get your job done."

I watched him as he put on a heavy coat, ski cap, gloves, and his warmest pair of shoes. He trudged out to the trash cans, looking like Nanook of the North, his breath visible like wisps of smoke. With a couple of trips back and forth, he completed the job before the city truck arrived and hauled everything away.

No, Matt didn't catch pneumonia. He didn't come down with the flu. And yes, I think he learned an important lesson.

Watching Matt from the window, I said to myself, "Lord, how many times will there be in his life when he doesn't want to do something or doesn't feel like doing something? Probably quite a few.

"How many people feel 100 percent gung-ho about their jobs all the time? Not too many. At one time or another, we all have responsibilities that we'd just as soon hand off to someone else." But if Matt has been given a job, he has to learn to carry it out. Unless he was running a temperature or hurting, unless he had come home from school and gone straight to bed without eating, he was healthy enough to take out the trash.

Matt has to learn about getting the job done correctly. It's part of life. It's part of being a man.

CHAPTER 12

The Value of Self-Discipline

The kind of self-discipline we're teaching our children at home is no different than self-discipline on the football field or at the office or, for that matter, in any aspect of life. Each of us has tasks to carry out. Each of us gets the job done.

When the Chicago Bears were at a peak in the mid 1980s, winning the Super Bowl in 1986, we had an unbeatable defense not only because of the talent of the players but because we all carried out our given assignments. We didn't freelance. We didn't take a day off. We had a plan to execute and we stuck with it. We demonstrated self-discipline.

Families have to work the same way, employing a disciplined game plan and approach to life. Everyone on the family team is given assignments to carry out. Shortcuts are unacceptable. Procrastination is not a viable option. We all work together and get things done.

Cleaning the Garage

I remember asking Matthew and Jill to clean out the garage one weekend afternoon last autumn. They were told to take everything out of the garage and clean it good. Granted, it was a pretty big job for two young kids (then 8 and 6). We, like most large families, have accumulated a lot of stuff. It wasn't an easy task, but I wanted to see how they would do.

I may have overestimated their ability. The job they did was acceptable, maybe, but certainly not great. "Is this it? Is this the best job you can do?" I asked them.

"No," they admitted.

"Okay, let's do it again," I said. "Do a job you would be proud of, not just enough to get by."

Their second effort was better—but the garage still wasn't as clean and orderly as it could have been. Bicycles were in the wrong place, a couple of tools were still lying outside the tool box, leaves and trash had collected in one of the corners.

Finally, with their third effort, Matt and Jill finished the job. "I want you to do your best, no matter what you are doing," I told them as I inspected their work. "When Daddy asks you to do something, I don't want to have to tell you more than one time. But don't expect Daddy to tell you everything. I want you to take it upon yourself to see everything that needs to be done gets done. Learn to anticipate things."

That's pretty standard advice I'd give to anyone assigned any kind of task—at home or at work. Go beyond what is expected. Seek out ways to do more.

Of course, if you challenge your children to do their best, you must first be committed to doing *your* best.

A Winner's Attitude

In many respects, being a parent is like being a coach. A coach's basic function is to motivate his or her charges to work their hardest and strive to do their best. Coaching (or parenting) isn't so much about all winning, per se, it's about developing a winner's attitude.

I remember watching one of Matthew's soccer games last fall, realizing that his mind was adrift. After we got home, I asked him, "Were you going all out during the game today?"

"Yes," he said.

"Well, it sure didn't seem like it," I remarked.

He shrugged. He might have known what was coming next. Advice from dear old Dad:

"Look, son, I don't care if you don't score any goals at all or make any great plays," I told him. "I don't care if you're the worst player on the whole team. I just want to see you hustling. I want to see you give your best effort. Because if you don't hustle, you're cheating yourself. God has given you a gift, son. I think you have more ability than I did as a kid—and that's fine. That's great. But whatever ability God has given you, I want you to say 'thank you' to God by doing your best. Honor him with your effort. That's all Daddy asks.

"In the classroom, in life, on the soccer field—whatever it is that you're doing, give it your best shot. I know sometimes you just want to have fun, and that's fine, too. Everything has its place. But when the coach or teacher is talking, I want you to listen. When it's time to play, go out and do your best. When it's time to study, hit the books hard.

"When it's time for recess, go out and have a great time. When we're sitting around the dinner table and we're joking, let's have fun. When we're fooling around, hey, let it fly. But you have to know what the situation is and act appropriately."

To be effective as a coach (or parent) you have to know your players (or children) and their limitations. What they can and cannot do. Try to put them in situations where they can figure out for themselves what needs to be done. That way, you help them find out what they are made of. With good coaching (parenting), you'll discover they are capable of more than you think.

Parents, especially Baby Boomer moms and dads, are notorious for taking the path of least resistance. We don't set up many rules and regulations for our kids to follow because we don't want the hassles or bickering that often ensues.

We're as likely to tell our children "Okay, fine, do your own thing" as we are to enforce discipline.

The irony of that is that children, for all their protestations and pouting, all their attempts to shirk their duties, actually crave that form of discipline in their lives. They want the structure and the rules. Because kids, who, I repeat, are no dummies, realize that when you establish rules and boundaries and announce your expectations for them, you are making an investment in their lives.

That investment is what kids want more than anything else: It's irrefutable proof that daddy and mommy care.

On the other hand, by refusing to add discipline and structure to their lives, you are tacitly saying to your children that they are not important enough to care about. You make them feel less confident in themselves, less secure.

Where parents also lack discipline is in using one of the simplest little words in the English language: capital N, capital O. *No*.

No, you can't have every new toy or game that reaches the marketplace. No, you can't have that Shaquille O'Neal jersey or those Michael Jordan shoes.

No, I don't care if everyone else in class will be there, you can't go to the slumber party at Johnny's or Janie's on Saturday night. No, you can't have those inline skates or that electric guitar just because the kids down the street have one.

On the other hand, I'm eager to say "Yes" to my children's requests. *If* they give their best effort in school, *if* they take good care of each other, *if* they show some initiative in their class projects.

Rewards and Incentives

I don't believe in something for nothing. I like rewards as much as the next person, but I want to earn them. I demand the satisfaction that comes with knowing that I put in the effort and made the sacrifices necessary to complete a task or reach a goal. Something for something, in other words.

Rewards and incentives have their place in the parenting process. Little kids are like big kids (adults); they need to have targets at which to aim. Kids need to see carrots dangling out in front of them at times. But I don't think parents should use incentives with children for things like household chores. Those responsibilities come with the territory. Besides, children need to look at household chores as opportunities to serve the family. Kids need to learn how to serve as well as to receive. I've seen how much my own children have grown from doing chores.

Kim and I try to accentuate the positive in our home. At times, rewards may take the form of going out for ice cream or perhaps a movie. Maybe we'll treat the kids by taking them to their favorite restaurant for dinner. But rewards and incentives don't necessarily have to involve big money. Sometimes, the best reward of all for a child is to hear daddy or mommy tell them, "I'm so excited about the job you've done. I had no idea you were going to do it that well. Man, that's terrific. I'm so proud of you."

To see the smiles on your children's faces when they receive heartfelt praise creates an unbelievable feeling of joy. Because you realize that inside their minds and hearts and souls they're saying to themselves, "Hey, I'm special."

We live in a world of instant gratification. People want things and they want them now. Many of us lack the patience or self-discipline to wait. Gimme this, gimme that. I gotta have it, can't wait, give it to me now.

You read about American consumers being awash in credit card debt, and you have to ask yourself, how much of that debt is related to parents who say yes to their children's every whim and wish? How much of debt is sheer overindulgence?

How much debt is a substitution for real love? How much is a lack of discipline?

Like it or not, we're living in a material world. Marketers have plenty of savvy, and they know how to reach kids with their selling messages—especially at Christmas.

But while a marketer's job is to push products at your children, a parent's job is to make sure discretionary expenditures fit into some overall family plan or budget and represent more than consumption for consumption's sake. That takes discipline on the part of mom and dad.

For example, last Christmas Kim and I imposed a limit on the number of gifts our children could receive from their relatives. We instructed their aunts and uncles to draw one name apiece. By doing that, we were able to reduce the greed factor and make each Christmas gift more special.

I know from my own experience how essential self-discipline is to an individual's development and growth. I wouldn't have been as successful in professional football without having the discipline to keep lifting weights when my muscles burned or running wind sprints when my chest heaved and my legs felt rubbery. I needed self-discipline to do all the daily pushups, pullups, and stretching exercises and to run "the hill."

Dads, we need to communicate to our children the value of having a disciplined approach in everything they do, from schoolwork to sports. We should strive to help our children make schedules and arrange their priorities.

The self-discipline required to make a game plan—and follow it—represents a great training exercise for children that can't begin too early in life.

CHAPTER 13

Spanking—Yes or No?

When family rules for conduct and behavior have been established, some form of punishment must exist for the occasions when children step over the line. Kids have to learn that actions have consequences.

If you mess up at the office (I'm talking about breaking company rules or policies), punishment might take the form of having your paycheck docked, or in extreme cases losing out on a promotion or even losing your job. If you mess up on the football field, punishment might take the form of having to run the stadium stairs or, in extreme cases, being benched or suspended. If you mess up at home, punishment might take the form of being grounded or receiving no allowance, or in extreme cases, being spanked.

Establishing Rules and Boundaries

What's the motivation for kids to behave at home if there's no swift and sure punishment? What good are the rules and boundaries in your household if there are no sanctions?

With our children, Kim and I heed the biblical admonition to "spare the rod and spoil the child." And, believe me, we have no intentions of raising spoiled children. Parents who don't discipline their kids do not demonstrate parental love.

On those infrequent occasions when I do have to administer a spanking—spanking being the last resort—I'll tell them, "This hurts me as much as it hurts you. But Daddy wouldn't be doing this if he didn't love you. This is because he cares for you so deeply." At times, I have cried right along with them.

Hey, being a dad is no picnic or day at the beach. It's tricky and complex. But fatherhood is the greatest responsibility I've ever been asked to handle. I'm responsible for loving, teaching, guiding, and affirming six children.

Do I like administering discipline to my children? No. I love having fun with them, playing around, and acting crazy and silly. I love horsing around with them—playing pony and having pillow fights. I love to play games or sit around and talk.

But I also know if I don't discipline them, if I don't teach the children right and wrong, if I don't set boundaries for their lives, someone else will. And that someone won't be anyone who loves them as much as their mother and I.

Some parents object to corporal punishment. Some find the mere thought of spanking to be repugnant and abhorrent. But I believe children can accept and cope with spanking more easily than another form of punishment—verbal abuse. Tell me which scenario is worse:

A. Parents who give their children a few pops on their bottom and then sit down to console their kids with words of reassurance.

B. Parents who do not spank their children, but instead scream at them: "You're no good. Worthless. I wish you had never been born. Now go to your room, I don't want to have to look at you. You make me sick. I hate you...."

Be Firm, But Flexible

With Kim's help, I've learned that spanking isn't the only form of punishment that can be instructive and still have the necessary impact. I confess that one of the most significant and positive changes in parenting since my childhood days is the adoption of techniques that defuse anger.

Techniques like calling time-out or having cool-off periods. Or sitting down with your children and explaining why some kind of reprimand, like cutting off privileges or "grounding" them from their favorite activities, is necessary.

When I was growing up, there wasn't much room for such negotiation with parents. If you messed up badly, you could expect a lickin' from dad or mom. There wasn't any individual counseling before the blows rained down, or any words of consolation afterward, either. All you could count on receiving was a sore behind.

Nowadays, spanking ranks way down the list as an option for punishment. It's pretty much become the court of last resort. Still the *threat* of spanking poses a meaningful disincentive to children.

The way in which parents decide to discipline their children has the potential to create serious problems in a marriage. With Kim's help and guidance, I was finally able to understand that the method I'd been exposed to—a swift and often violent spanking—wasn't the best, or only, way to resolve things.

Years ago, when our oldest three children were fairly young, I took the lead in family discipline. I told Kim, "Okay, look, I'm going to handle things my way. I know kids and I know the way you have to deal with them."

For a while, Kim went along with me, even though I probably went overboard enforcing rules and regulations. I was as tough and inflexible as Captain Bligh or one of those military martinets.

Finally, exercising her love and patience, Kim brought me to grips with a potentially troubling situation. She said, "Mike, I love you very much, but our kids are afraid of you. They're intimidated. They're saying what they think you want to hear, instead of telling the truth. They're just saying things to please you. What's going to happen in a few years is that we're never going to know the truth."

That was hard for me to hear. I wanted Kim to tell me how great a job I was doing as a disciplinarian. Hey, when I said something, the kids hopped to it.

Instead, she was crying softly and telling me she was worried because the kids feared their father. That I was overbearing and domineering.

"Mike, if we lose our children now," Kim said, "their teenage years will be unbearable."

Kim's remarks really hit a nerve. She was right: for a long time, all I wanted to hear from the children were the right things. "Yes, sir, you're right" or "Yes, sir, I understand" or "Yes, sir, I will not do that again."

I had to take a step back and grasp what Kim was saying about my actions toward our children. I'd always taken great pride in how our children obeyed mommy and daddy. I'd always been proud to show off their behavior around their grandparents or other relatives. But that was my pride. The regimentation I imposed was filling a need in me, not in my children.

I had to get my outlook turned 180 degrees and look at the situation from my kids' perspective. I had to consider their self-esteem and their feelings. I didn't want to be a controlling father or an intimidating presence in their lives. I didn't want them to be afraid to tell me the truth.

New Methods of Discipline

About three or four years ago, with Kim's encouragement, I went down another path with the discipline of our children. When problems came up and punishment was called for, I began asking: "Kristen, what do you think about this?" Or "Jill, what do you think we should do?"

Sometimes the self-punishment they suggested was more severe than anything I had planned.

I remember last year asking Jill what kind of punishment she deserved for a rules infraction and she piped up, "Daddy, I won't eat for three days." When I suggested that might not be very practical, she said, "Okay, I won't go outside for three weeks."

"That might be overdoing it just a bit," I told her. We reached a reasonable compromise.

While learning about discipline, I also learned another important lesson: Dads don't have to be infallible. Dads can admit their mistakes. There have been occasions when I've had to say, "Kids, Daddy made a mistake. I was too hard on you. I'm sorry. I'll know better next time."

Believe me, that was a difficult thing for me to learn to do. It wasn't anything I knew about. I'd grown up in a world where daddy could do no wrong. He was omnipotent. When he said jump, you asked "how high?" Then you jumped.

Led by Kim's example, we have become more creative with our discipline for the children. We rely on more alternatives than the proverbial trip to the woodshed.

A Different Punishment

One time last year when I was away on business, Matthew and Jill had a little fracas. I'd previously had a long talk with Matthew about his role when I am away. "When I go out of town on business, son, you have to be the man of the house. You have to protect all the women. You have to listen to what Mom says and you have to show your love for your sisters."

"I can do that, Dad," he pledged.

Now there I was on the telephone hearing about how Matt had lost it and gone Rambo on his little sister.

"You know what," I said to Kim. "I'm going to have to spank him for that."

"No, Mike," Kim responded. "Spanking's not the answer. I know something that will leave a more lasting impression."

Kim knew that Matt had been eagerly looking forward to going over to a friend's house on Friday afternoon after school.

"Mike, we'll tell him that he can't go," she said. "That will do it. He'll realize how serious we are about having him treat Jill with respect."

"That's not going to do any good," I snorted. "All he's going to say is 'Wow, I'm not going to get a spanking.'"

Kim shook her head. "Believe me, he will be upset," she predicted. "This will hurt him more than you can imagine."

"Sweetheart, you're letting Matthew off too easy," I disagreed. "But if you think that's the way to handle it, I'm going to go along with you."

She was right. When I got back home and together we broke the news to Matthew that he couldn't go to his friend's house after school, he burst into tears. I mean this guy was in agony. His eyes were gushing like Niagara Falls; he could have raised the water table in Lake Michigan.

"Why can't I go?" he sobbed. "What did I do?"

We patiently explained to Matthew why he was being punished. We told him he might be able to play at his friend's in the future—if he corrected his mistake and apologized to his sister.

Kim's awareness of that particular situation and her understanding of the most meaningful punishment to impose is an example of being close enough to your children to read them and study them.

That's another reason why daddy has to be home: If he doesn't know his children well enough and is unable to realize what's important to them, he's going to make some unnecessary mistakes.

Establishing the Rules

The key to administering punishment is being consistent. Parents can't change the rules all the time. I don't think that's fair. They have to establish what the rules are and communicate them clearly.

For example, I will tell our children, "Daddy's going to tell you to do this [say, make up your bed] one time, then I expect you to do it. I don't want to have to lecture you about it and I don't want to drive myself crazy repeating it. So I'll just tell you one time, okay? If you don't do it, I'm going to grab your shoulder and squeeze. And that's going to hurt."

Kim and I aren't trying to pull their shoulders out of joint. A squeeze is something that's uncomfortable and gets their attention.

In general, the procedure for administering discipline at our house goes something like this: For a first offense, we tell the kids not to do that again. The second time, we squeeze their shoulder. For a third offense, they are grounded. For a fourth offense, depending on the situation and how serious the offense, spanking becomes an alternative. We seldom reach level four.

When we spank the children, we take them into my office, get out a wooden spoon, and swat their bottom a couple of times. Then we'll say: "Hey, I love you. I'm disappointed in what happened. I'm sorry about your behavior, but by no means am I disappointed in you. You're still a champion in my book."

The reason Kim and I use a wooden spoon for spanking is twofold: one, we want our own hands only associated with loving touches; two, because of the strength in my hands, I could hurt them even unintentionally.

Daddy and mommy must be a team in the punishment phase as well as the rule-setting phase. They can't send mixed signals to their kids. They have to stand together in a united front in discipline. That's part of showing family leadership and teamwork.

In return, children will honor their parents by demonstrating the discipline that's been instilled in them. Kids do so not out of fear but out of mutual respect for their parents.

I can't tell you how many times, after airplane trips, people have come up to me or Kim and said, "When I saw your whole family trooping down the aisle I thought we were going to be in for a dreadful experience. But your children, they are so … *well-behaved.*"

We are flattered, naturally, to hear such comments. They come about because we take the time to talk to our children and establish ground rules for appropriate behavior. Our children show their love for us—and their respect—by following those rules. That's what discipline is all about.

CHAPTER 14

Dads and Marriages Don't Always Mix

Before dad can earn his stripes as a leadership partner and disciplinarian—creating the legacy of love so essential to his children—he first has to devote himself to being a great husband.

How is that supposed to happen if dad's focus is beyond the family or if he has one foot out the door? It won't.

A Nation of Divorcees

Roughly fifty percent of the marriages in America today end in divorce. Let me repeat that—*fifty* percent of American marriages fail. That makes every wedding ceremony a coin flip: Heads the bride and groom stay together, tails they don't. Call it in the air.

Is anybody else shocked by that statistic? Outraged? What is going on in society? The institution of marriage is intended to be the most sacred of unions, the holiest of bonds. Spouses aren't supposed to be as disposable as, say, soft drink bottles or AA batteries.

Kim and I have been married almost thirteen years, and already we've seen friends from college and the Chicago Bears end first marriages and start a second. A few friends are already on their third marriage.

A fifty-percent divorce rate represents immeasurable stress and conflict for people to deal with and work through. It also explains why so many American children grow up in single-parent homes. Or why children grow up living with one biological parent and a stepfather or stepmother (some of whom care more about their spouses than the stepkids). And why other kids are forced to live in foster homes or with legal guardians. There's a whole generation of American children who've grown up having no relationship whatsoever with their biological father.

We've seen a social cost for dad's absence paid in drug use, runaways, pregnancies, and other sobering statistics.

What Happened?

Divorce rates in America remained below 10 percent through the late 1950s and early 1960s, then shot up in the 1970s and 1980s. Not coincidentally, this sea change occurred concurrently with the sexual revolution and the rise of the women's movement. It also occurred about the time that participation in weekly church services began declining and some people began promoting the notion that God was dead.

Once a sort of declaration of independence with stigmatizing side effects, divorce became chic, hip, the "trendy" thing to do. Within the legal profession, divorce attorneys found so much demand for their services that some became celebrities.

Part of the rise in divorce rates probably reflected adults who, after years together raising the children, discovered they had grown apart. Finding the nest empty, they decided to fly off in separate directions.

Part of the increase coincided with the women's liberation movement that began in the 1960s and accelerated through the 1970s. Women simply got tired of being mistreated or neglected at home by insensitive mates. Some women got tired of being whupped on. Unlike their mothers and grandmothers, who withstood the abuse by turning the other cheek, they willingly stepped out of bad situations. They renounced their second-class citizenship. Bravo for them.

At the same time, men began to exhibit less fidelity. Or perhaps their infidelity became more blatant. Some men ditched their longtime partners for younger, so-called trophy wives. Other men spent so much time at the office trying to climb the corporate ladder that their eyes began wandering toward colleagues and co-workers.

Spurred by a number of these factors, each gender apparently became less committed to the institution of marriage. The pledge to love each other "until death do us part" fell out of favor and was replaced by the pledge to love each other until "three years or 30,000 miles," whichever comes first. Not quite, but you get my point.

Some people shrug their shoulders and say, "So what if more people are getting divorced? That's no big deal. It's better to divorce than stay in a harmful, counterproductive relationship."

I disagree. Divorce is a *huge* deal. Divorce needs to be the court of last resort for married couples, not the first place to turn in the face of a crisis.

God hates divorce. He understands the repercussions when families are split apart. As the Creator, who put the pieces of the family puzzle together in the first place, he knows that when he isn't the glue, everything is fragile and can easily fall apart. That's why a major priority for any couple should be establishing a relationship with the Lord.

Who pays the price for this fracturing of the family unit? To some degree the husband and wife (although in many cases one or both of them will have a prospective replacement waiting in the wings). The brunt of the blow, however, is borne by children.

Children of divorced couples suddenly have to cope with having only a single parent. These kids have to sort out their feelings about abandonment, about being deserted by their flesh and blood. It's children who pay the ultimate price of divorce.

I can't say for sure what percentage would represent a reasonable divorce rate in America—10 percent? 20 percent? perhaps as much as 25 percent?—but I can say with certainty that 50 percent is too high. It's preposterous. And it's damaging to our youth.

Making Marital Mistakes

I know as human beings we can't help making mistakes. Sometimes our mistakes show up in the form of faulty judgment when we pick a mate. I know one divorcee stung by her faulty selections so often she says, "If you were to line up fifty eligible bachelors against a wall, all of them seemingly decent and honorable men, give me just ten minutes and I guarantee I would zero in on the biggest loser in the bunch. And then proceed to fall in love with him."

Regardless of mistakes people make, the divorce problem is simply too big and its effects are too great to ignore. We need to consider possible solutions.

One possible course of action would be to make divorces harder to obtain. Before couples could end a marriage, for example, require them to undergo professional counseling sessions geared to working out their difficulties.

Or maybe states and municipalities should require a "cooling off" period between the time a couple files for divorce and when the divorce is granted. None of this flying out to Reno or Las Vegas for a "quickie" divorce. In the interim, every effort should be geared to promoting reconciliation.

On the other hand, why wait until marriages are on shaky ground to take action? How about if we did more at the front-end of a prospective marriage, with pre-marriage counseling?

Perhaps couples should undergo compatability tests before receiving a wedding license. Maybe a team of marriage counselors could help couples evaluate their likelihood of growing together. If states can mandate that citizens take a test before they issue a driver's license, maybe they should require couples to take a wedding skills test before they issue a wedding license. There's no doubt whatsoever that more people have been harmed by failed marriages than by automobile accidents.

Picking a Partner

I'd suggest compatability tests be based on basic issues about values. How important to your prospective partner are issues such as family, children, money, status, ambition? What is the role of religion in your life? Are you a believer? Do you worship regularly? What do you see as the purpose of your life? What are some of your goals? What are you working toward?

Go down a checklist. Answers to these and similar questions won't eliminate all bad pairings or mismatches of men and women, but such a test might give prospective marriage partners some idea of whether they are suited to each other.

The first step toward finding a partner is to understand that person's nature and character. The signs are unmistakable if you look for them:

- Does she have self-esteem and self-respect?
- Is he charitable and friendly toward others?
- Is she selfish and egocentric?

- Even if he has a quiet nature and reserved temperament (we're not all outgoing types), does he have a positive outlook on life, or is he grouchy and grumpy, always complaining and whining about the world?
- Does she have so much excess baggage that you need a bellhop or redcap to deal with the load?
- How well does this person stand up to adversity? Does she/he deal with it on a mature level? Or does she/he practice the art of denial, choosing not to deal with adversity and pretending nothing has happened? Does she/he let setbacks get her/him down, or does she/he bounce off the canvas and continue the fight?
- Is this person honorable? Does she have ethics and integrity? Does she take the blame when she is at fault or point the finger at others? Does she make excuses, or get things done?
- How committed is this person to growth? What are his interests and activities? Does he use his talents or squander them by just going through the motions of living? Is his a life of inspiration or dissipation?
- What role does religion play in this person's life? Does she have a relationship with God? Does she have her own identity in Christ?

Of course, answering these questions doesn't guarantee you a perfect spouse or a problem-free marriage, but the information you gain will help you and your prospective mate decide if you are compatible enough to commit to each other for life.

Money Matters

Because so many marriages in America dissolve because of disputes over finances, we would be well-advised to evaluate how a prospective marriage partner regards money. The key issue isn't earning power, either. The cogent question, rather, is how do they handle the income they have? I know of no correlation between income and marital harmony. Some of the poorest people make the best marriage partners; some of the richest people make the worst.

Observe a prospective marriage partner. Based on your observations, how would you answer the following questions?

- Is he a conspicuous consumer?
- Does she live beyond her means?
- Does he have a sense of thrift?
- Does she have a monthly budget?
- Does he run up massive credit card debts?
- Does she spend in reckless fashion?
- Does he have contingency funds for emergencies?
- Does she have the discipline to delay gratification in discretionary purchases?

Those are just some of the critical questions that have to be answered before you can accurately gauge another person's character. Those are some of the checkpoints for seeing a prospective marriage partner as she or he really is—not as you wish them to be. (It's funny, so many people enter a marriage believing they can "change" their spouse. Yes, a person can change temporarily, according to circumstances, but those changes will be short-lived. Only God can change what's in a person's heart.)

Those answers will tell you if there's a mesh of your collective beings.

Kim and I

I'm grateful to have the blessing of Kim as my wife and partner. She has made me a better person and, in doing so, has given me the chance to be a better father.

I knew from virtually the first time we met that she had been heaven sent. A gift from God. She possessed an inner beauty and strength that was undeniable. Her approach to life was straightforward and honest, with no guile or manipulation or deceit. She was pure in heart, mind, and body. She was the product of a warm and loving family. She was a giver, not a taker.

She was always herself. She didn't put on airs or try to be anything she wasn't. She was beautiful from the inside out, which made her special in my eyes. She was real, not a phony.

She was the first woman around whom I could relax and just be me. I didn't have to strut around like a super jock or try to use any of the cheap lines I'd read in books or heard in songs.

I could sit with her on a picnic blanket and talk about how green the grass was and how much blue was in the sky. I could talk to her about feeling lonely or misunderstood. I could talk to her about missing my brother Grady, who was dead, about missing my dad, who just wasn't there.

We spent the many months (and years) of our extended courtship getting to know each other well. We grew together spiritually. After a while, we came to know each other inside and out.

We weren't, as many newlyweds discover to their horror, strangers. Our relationship wasn't based on physical pleasure, which many kids mistakenly make the centerpiece of their couplehood. You might as well base a marriage on a mutual affinity for key lime pie as base it on a mutual affinity for sex.

Total Commitment Required

What kind of person makes the right marriage partner? That can be difficult to nail down. You've heard the adage that opposites attract, so that theory has its proponents. But others will argue that it's imperative for a husband and wife to see eye-to-eye on all the key issues: religion, politics, child-raising, money management. They may be right. I also think it's safe to say that all relationships should be built on mutual respect and trust.

In my opinion, what makes marriage work is a total commitment to each other. It's about selflessness—the same kind of "family first" attitude I described earlier—and servanthood.

When dad's focus is on family—his spouse and children—it's virtually impossible to be distracted or sidetracked by the job, by another person, by other interests. It's hard to misplace your priorities. Those other things, while important, take on secondary roles in his life.

In my opinion, one reason so many marriages fail is the other side of the same coin: the attitude of "me first." It's selfishness expressed in a lack of commitment to your partner and an unwillingness to sacrifice your private agenda to meet the needs of someone else. Someone you profess to "love."

Most of us don't recognize initially how demanding marriage will be. I know I didn't. I had no idea that marriage could turn me into a hypocrite, liar, and breaker of promises—all of which I quickly became. I had no idea of the price you have to pay to learn what love is all about.

Keep in mind, I had a great supportive partner helping me. How arduous is that struggle for personal growth if you have to go it alone?

Someone needs to be a messenger about marriage, so I'll volunteer. I'll gladly tell young men and women how tough marriage will be. One of the best pieces of advice about marriage I can offer is this: The Lord has to be the most important aspect of your life (with your spouse second). The same goes for your spouse. She or he must put God first and keep you second, because any person who keeps God first will treat a spouse as she or he deserves to be treated. You will grow together as one, under God, and develop a love that surpasses understanding.

Let me tell you: It's hard for a marriage to grow apart when you work together as one. Kim and I are on the same page because we know what the family vision is, we know what the mission statement says and we know what the family goals are.

As parents and marriage partners, we leave nothing to chance.

CHAPTER 15

Why Marriage Works for This Dad

One of the recurring themes in this book is the positive influence Kim has had on my performance as a husband and father. She made me realize that I was spending too much time apart from her and our children—mentally and physically. She forced me to deal with my autocratic tendencies and the strictness and harshness in my tone. Kim also made me focus on forgiveness.

Those changes not only made me a better family leader, they strengthened our marriage. Through communication, we've been able to address—and resolve—issues that might have undermined our family. Our evolution together has given our children more hope for the future, because we've been able to do a better job as parents.

In the Beginning

When I met Kim, I immediately recognized her honesty and humanity, her energy and zest for life. I could see her seriousness as a student and the organized process by which she carried out her tasks.

I could tell she possessed a good sense of humor, which wasn't my strongest suit. She was able to get me to lighten up a little bit, to relax, to not be so serious and grave. She taught me how to laugh and have a good time. If you were to drop in, you'd often find us joking and laughing. Just having a ball together.

Kim comes from a large and loving family and she transmitted that warmth to everyone she encountered. She is vivacious and outgoing, and she drew me out of my reservations and inhibitions.

We spent hours and hours talking about life, sharing our views and feelings on many of life's most important issues.

When did I know I had fallen in love with Kim? I don't think there was one exact, revelatory moment when the clouds parted, a ray of sunlight burst down from the heavens, and a deep voice intoned, "Mike, Kim's the one for you."

I'm not sure I went to sleep one night and in a dream saw Kim as an angel with wings, beckoning me to follow her on the pathway to the promised land. I don't recall an instant when my heart fluttered, or I felt feverish, or my skin broke out in goosebumps.

But I realized I loved Kim wholeheartedly and wanted to devote my life to her. That realization evolved as I came to know her inner self: that she had a commitment to family first; that she had an active, engaged Christian faith; that she was a giver, not a taker; that she was unselfish.

Kim also was at peace with her total being. She had the courage to fall in love with a man of a different race, a decision that would eventually ostracize her from some on our small, conservative college campus. She could anticipate some of the hurdles our union would set before us: a mixed-race marriage, children of mixed color, cold stares from some people on the street, words of rebuke and disapproval from others.

She never broke stride.

Our Early Years in Marriage

We talked and prayed a great deal in the early years of our marriage about setting the right example of a loving parental relationship for the children we were planning to have. As you know, I had grown up in an environment where my parents were often at odds with each other. Their conflict filled our household with negative energy; it was too pronounced to miss, as prominent as the sofa or television set. Consequently, I had not witnessed the loving example children need to see from both parents, as Kim had. My positive influence primarily had been my mother.

As parents, you simply cannot talk to your children about how daddy loves mommy and mommy loves daddy, and then act in a contradictory fashion. You can't talk the talk of marital accord, you have to walk the walk. Kids are perceptive enough to sniff out insincerity like a hound sniffs out its quarry. Which is not to suggest that as loving partners you will not have disputes and disagreements. Show me parents that never argue, or live together totally without discord, and I'll submit their names to the *Guinness Book of World Records.* They'll be the first in human history.

Conflicts and Resolution

One of my teammates on the Chicago Bears once told me that, growing up, he never saw his mom and dad have a single disagreement. When he was a newlywed, however, he and his new bride were constantly bickering.

This guy was going crazy, thinking he was an utter failure as a husband. Finally, he picked up the phone and called his father. "Dad, you wouldn't believe it, we're fighting all the time," he said. "How come you and Mom never acted like this? What am I doing wrong?"

"You're not doing anything wrong, son," his father replied. "Believe me, your mother and I had plenty of disagreements. More than you'll ever know. But we decided when we started having babies that we would never argue in front of the kids. And we kept that promise."

When we heard that story, Kim and I pledged to settle our conflicts in the open. When we disagree, we make sure our children see us work things out. We want them to be aware what a loving relationship looks like and sounds like. We want them to see arguments settled without rancor or recrimination. Or any aftershocks. (Of course, there are some issues so private—or that the children wouldn't understand—that we settle behind closed doors.)

How parents handle those inevitable moments of friction is of paramount importance. The examples of behavior children see and hear during parental arguments dramatically influence how they will resolve their own conflicts and disputes in years to come. Children are great imitators, and will follow a parent's lead; so, dads, be careful what you say and do. If words spit out during an argument are hurtful, malicious, and abusive, they will leave a lasting negative impression.

I recommend that parents take the time after any parental spat or argument the children are aware of to make sure the kids understand that the conflict was temporary and its source was addressed and resolved. Don't leave your kids out of the loop, wondering: Does Daddy still love Mommy (or vice versa)? Did he really mean it when he raised his voice like that? Gee, is our family falling apart? If it does, what will happen to me?

Give your children closure before any doubts arise. Then move on.

Our children have never had cause to be confused like that. They know their mommy and daddy are totally committed to each other. They've heard one or the other of us say, on many occasions, "You know what? I don't agree with you, but if that's how you feel, that's what we'll do. We're a team. So I'll go along with you."

Transparency

One giant step toward being a better husband—and, by extension, father—is making yourself transparent. A real man expresses his love by letting his spouse see inside him, to the deepest level. He trusts her enough to let her see through him. He drops the sacred guy-code of being noncommunicative.

A real man is not afraid to talk about topics deeper than the safe stuff: football teams, current events, where you'd like to go for vacation, your favorite movie or restaurant, your idea of the perfect meal.

A real man strips away protective layers and exposes himself. He reveals his relationship with Jesus Christ. His relationship with other people. His hurts and pains. His worries and neuroses. His disappointments. His fears.

He keeps nothing hidden. He brings out the skeletons in his closet. He puts his flaws and faults on the table.

By being transparent, a real man creates true intimacy with his spouse and in so doing, establishes deeper levels of trust and understanding. His willingness to open up and stand emotionally naked before her will foster a new devotion between them.

Her burdens become his, and he'll help find solutions to problems and work out resolutions. He will, literally, become a new man: ready to pitch in and help with anything from cooking and cleaning to doing the laundry. Together, they will form a "can do" attitude that cannot be overcome.

A real man's transparency ensures his fidelity. He will gain the resolve to remain pure and faithful to his wife no matter how alluring the devil in a blue dress appears to be. He'll acquire the self-discipline not to submit to temptation. He will exercise the self-control suggested by the phrase "forsaking all others."

Transparency enables a real man to direct his passion to marriage and the offspring his marriage produces. Primarily, transparency enables a man to love his wife through service, as Jesus loved the church. He will make any sacrifice necessary for her. If need be, he will die for her.

A real man doesn't act like the master of the universe. He doesn't get caught up in trying to be the absolute authority of the household, who always has the final say. Father may know best about some things, but not all.

Too many marriages have come undone because the man has overplayed his hand. He's taken the position that he's in total control, that his needs must be met first, that everything and everyone else must be subordinate to him. A real man's love for a woman isn't about being a master, but a servant. Serving her needs with all the resources at his command.

As I frequently remind my children, "Your mommy's the champion in this household. She's the hardest worker by far. She has the most difficult job keeping everything around here moving and on track. Your responsibility, and mine, is to do everything we can to make things easier for her. Whatever else happens around here, we have to help lighten Mom's load. Got it?"

An Awakening

I discovered the role I needed to fill as husband and father late one night after a disagreement with Kim. We had quarreled and she had gone to bed upset.

I was sitting up in the den, trying to analyze the situation. Why had we fought that evening? Why couldn't she see things my way? I felt extremely frustrated.

"You say you love me, Mike," she had said as the argument escalated. "But it comes with a string attached. What you mean is 'I love you, if'—*if* you agree with me. You're always asking for my opinion about everything, but when my opinion isn't the same as yours, you don't want to hear it."

Somewhere, I had fallen off track. Was I loving her the right way? I felt that I didn't have a clue. As the hours went by, I started flipping through the Bible, searching for some consolation. Some guidance.

There, in the wee hours of the morning, I found an answer. Overcome with joy, I raced upstairs to tell her. I shook her gently and she stirred.

"Mike, do you know what time it is?" she asked. "It's after 3 o'clock."

"I don't care. I want you to read this. This is how I'm going to love you for the rest of our lives."

"I'll read it in the morning," she said, rolling back over.

"No," I insisted. "You have to hear it now."

The answer was in the first book of Corinthians. "Listen to this, Kim," I said and began reading:

> "Love is patient, love is kind. It does not envy, it does not boast, it is not proud. It is not rude, it is not self-seeking, it is not easily angered, it keeps no record of wrongs. Love does not delight in evil but rejoices with the truth. It always protects, always trusts, always hopes, always perseveres" (13:4–7).

I told Kim that was how I would love her from that day forward. That was almost eight years ago. That was when I learned the meaning of real love. Sad to say, I had read that passage many times before, but this was the first time I really grasped its meaning.

From that point forward, I began to change as a husband and father. It was an awakening.

CHAPTER 16

Stages in a Marriage

At many of the presentations I make to a leadership series sponsored by the Gallup organization, I discuss marriages and emphasize the role fathers play in each of the three distinct stages, or phases—Lovers, Associates, and Roommates.

I'll go to a blackboard and draw five large circles below each of the three words. These circles represent family goals, career goals, social goals, personal development, and spiritual growth.

"Throughout your adult life, these are the five areas that are likely foremost in importance," I'll say to the participants. "Let's look at how they pertain to marriage."

Lovers

Stage one of a marriage I call the "lovers" or "honeymooners" phase. It spans roughly the first five years. "This is the ideal state of marriage," I'll say. "Husband and wife can't get enough of each other. Their days and nights are characterized by bliss. They're getting established in their jobs. They're looking at buying a first home and contemplating having children. This period is what you might call their own private version of 'Happy Days.'

"Notice how the circles are overlapped," I'll say, "just as their lives are intertwined. They are functioning as a unit, a

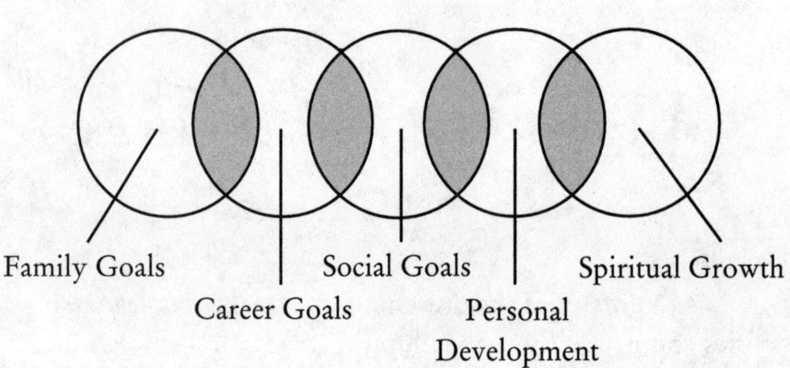

team. They are melded in heart and soul. The husband is totally absorbed in his wife—and vice versa. They have no secrets. They share a total commitment to each other."

Time has a way of changing things, of course. Change is one of the constants in our life. Tomorrow will be different from today, and accepting that fact—anticipating and managing change—is crucial for dad and mom.

Associates

During years five to fifteen, a marriage typically evolves into a new phase as pressures—both external and internal—begin to mount. "I call stage two the 'Associates' phase of marriage," I'll explain. "It's probably the most common stage my wife and I see among our peers. We feel the same pressures they do.

"The married couple we were describing in stage one now has several children running around the house. The kids are darling. They're smart and cute and well-behaved—little angels, to tell the truth—but they begin to impede on the family schedule. They have soccer games to play, piano lessons or cheerleading practice in the afternoon, Scout meetings to attend. The children have become so busy they need a private shuttle service.

"Meanwhile, Dad's busy in his career. He's trying to climb the corporate ladder, and he's spending more time at the office. He has to wrestle with the dilemma of balancing work assignments and family responsibility.

"Mom, meanwhile, is either on the same career track with her work, or she has made the choice to stay home and attend to the children. If it's the latter situation, she's probably harried and stressed out by all the daily juggling of schedules."

I'll step up to the blackboard again and draw five more circles. This time, the circles touch, but do not overlap.

Associates Stage
(young children)

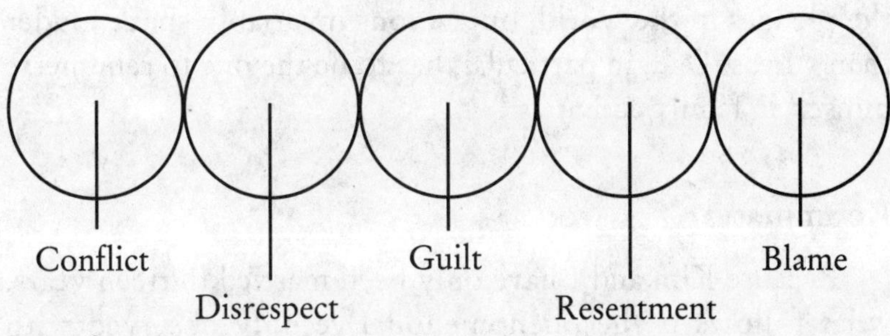

"When the children's needs and concerns are overlaid on the marriage, the circles take on new meaning. Now the five circles represent things like conflict, disrespect, guilt, resentment, blame.

"Dad and mom are starting to act more like associates than lovers or honeymooners. The ardor has cooled and the passion has waned. Disagreements in the household have become more frequent. A tug-of-war ensues between dad and mom over whose needs are more urgent and whose career is more important." Almost without fail, one or the other will start to form a grudge because they feel they're getting the short end of the stick.

I'll tap chalk lightly on the blackboard. "Notice how the circles are now merely touching—they are no longer intertwined. This represents the probability that man and woman are starting to grow apart from each other. They are starting to think about 'Me' more than 'We.'

"Dad often begins making plans that don't always include his wife and children. He begins flirting with danger—or perhaps with some colleague at his office.

"At this point, it's still possible for a married couple to return to the 'Lovers' stage," I say, "but only if dad and mom make a renewed commitment to each other. That's not always easy to do, either, because it requires candor and transparency. It means admitting mistakes, which many people find hard to do.

"Lip service alone won't cut it, though. You can make all the pledges in the world, but actions invariably speak louder than words. Dad, in particular, has to be the one to reimmerse himself in family activities."

Roommates

Because Kim and I have only been married thirteen years, what follows is the phenomenon I've only observed with many of my closest friends, who are in their late forties and early fifties.

"Somewhere after fifteen or so years in a marriage, couples enter stage three," I'll say, while drawing five separate circles on the blackboard. "I refer to this as the 'Roommates' phase. Dad and mom are still living under the same roof, but they keep separate agendas. They're pretty much doing their own thing. They've put career matters or other considerations ahead of family matters."

The circles are now separated because direction and focus in the relationship have been lost. The ideals of personal

Roommates Stage
(older children)

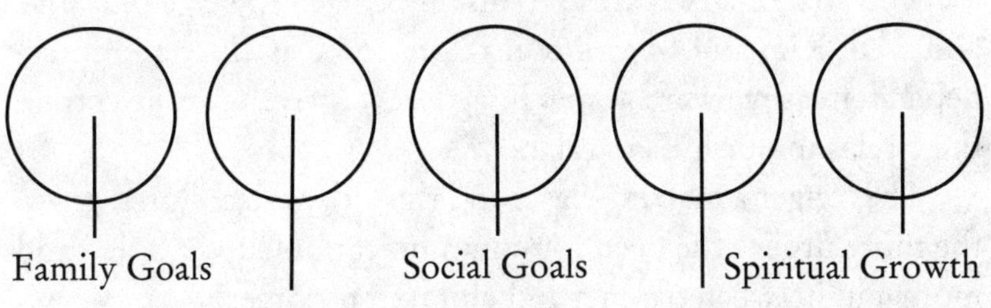

growth and spiritual growth have been submerged. The blame and resentment issues subside as an unspoken truce is declared.

"Note that the circles no longer touch. That's because dad and mom are now living apart—like *islands*. They've lost contact with each other and with their children. Everyone in the household is going in separate directions, doing his or her own thing.

"The family doesn't sit down together for meals, where they can talk and share experiences. Family time is infrequent. Discipline is missing. The kids, now teenagers, have no curfew. They're out running around, doing who knows what. Mom and dad have surrendered their authority, and teenagers are being influenced, more likely than not, by peer pressure.

"The family is just trying to get by. It has few ambitions beyond getting the kids into college or into a trade school or vocational program that offers some prospect for employment. Other than that, mom and dad are just hoping the kids don't break the law or run away or smash the family car. They're just trying to survive with as little damage as possible.

"This kind of dynamic ruins many lives and families," I'll say. "I've seen it over and over again in my life. When couples reach the roommates stage, divorce begins to loom as a reasonable, perhaps inevitable, consequence."

Overlapping Lives

The goal of any marriage should be to keep stage one alive and well. Kim and I work constantly to be as close and interdependent as we were as newlyweds. We strive to make certain the circles in our lives overlap.

The longer a marriage lasts and the older the children grow, the more urgent the need for communication between dad and mom and between parents and children becomes.

Normally, however, what happens is the opposite: Couples stop communicating with each other and go underground with their true feelings. Rather than try to talk to their spouse, who doesn't seem to be listening, dads and moms start confiding in their friends. They start talking to coworkers. Kids, instead of talking to their parents, start talking to peers.

Renewing Wedding Vows

I think that one way to ensure that parents don't become islands unto themselves is for married couples to renew their wedding vows. A church service, with family members and friends attending, would be great. So would a private ceremony in your own home or backyard. It doesn't have to be expensive or elaborate.

That kind of commitment will give dad and mom a new level of trust in each other, as well as a renewed sense of purpose to face life's problems head-on. Refocusing on marriage will give dad and mom confidence in all their actions together.

If marriage partners are able to reach new levels of understanding through communication and commitment, they will create more underpinning for the family. In turn, they will be able to serve as better leaders of their children. Which is what parenting is really all about.

CHAPTER 17

Teach Your Children Well

By now, I hope I've persuaded fathers to rededicate themselves to family and to score their greatest triumphs at home by serving their spouses and children.

Some fathers, however, might still be asking: What exactly should I teach my children?

I can't create a lesson plan for every couple or every single parent to follow—nor would I be presumptuous enough to try. But there are twelve life lessons Kim and I work ceaselessly to impart to our children:

1. Finish the Race
2. Do Your Best
3. Tell the Truth
4. Be Humble
5. Life Isn't Fair
6. Be Responsible for Your Choices
7. Lead by Example
8. Have Courage
9. Live Your Dreams
10. Respect Yourself
11. Expect the Best
12. Be Disciplined

These twelve lessons can't be covered in a period of days or weeks. Or even months or years. Your children have to absorb these lessons through frequent family discussions, as well as periodic family reviews and evaluations. These lessons require training and reinforcement. They are, in fact, the kind of lessons dads and moms must teach on an everyday basis, which helps explain why parenting is an ongoing job.

I'll say it again: parenthood entails no down time. There are no holidays or vacations or days off. Parenthood is a full-time, hands-on, systematic process.

Let's examine each of these twelve life lessons—which Kim and I have been devising and refining over the years—more closely.

1. Finish the Race

Making a commitment to finish whatever you start requires discipline, not to mention delaying or postponing gratification. By being committed to finishing any race or job, a person ensures he or she will not back down from challenges or take shortcuts or seek the easy way out. By adhering to this policy, a person will develop character and confidence.

A few years ago, for example, Matthew expressed an interest in ice skating. He had seen up close how much fun his sister Kristen was having in picking up skating skills. We enrolled him in a beginner's class, but after a couple sessions at the rink, Matt decided he'd had enough. He wasn't going to be the next Scott Hamilton or Elvis Stojko.

"I don't want to skate anymore," he announced one night at the dinner table. "I just don't like it."

"Well, after you go ahead and finish with your lessons, then we'll see about getting you involved in something else," I replied. "But first you're going to finish the class. You're not going to say that you want to do something and then quit the minute you discover you don't like it as much as you expected. There are no quitters in this family. You'll complete your series of lessons, simple as that. If you want to do something else afterward, fine. That's your decision. Your mom and I will be all for it. We'll support you 100 percent. But quitting skating now isn't an option. You will see it through, and then we'll look at other activities."

I'm not picking on Matthew. We went through the same thing with Kristen. She had been eager to learn piano, but once we arranged for lessons and she saw how much time was involved with practicing the scales and repetitions, her heart was back at the playground. "I want to be outside, playing with my friends," she insisted. "Sure thing, honey," I told her. "As soon as you finish all the lessons we've arranged."

We impressed on her the same thing we impressed on our son: Whatever you choose to do, see it through. Anybody can start a race, but not everybody can finish.

2. Do Your Best

We address this attitude in our family's mission statement. Doing your best in any endeavor you undertake represents one way of saying thanks to God.

As I tell our children, do your best, but don't be overly concerned with winning. And don't get wrapped up in thinking about yourself, or how many awards you'll win, or how much applause or recognition you will receive. Keep your ego in check.

Just put your nose to the grindstone and go to work. Decide what it takes to be the best you can possibly be, then strive with all your heart and might to accomplish that one thing.

I don't care whether we're talking about building a better mousetrap or making the highest score on the college boards. Just give it your all.

This past year, Kristen qualified for the spelling bee at her elementary school. As she studied for the final competition, I suggested she go over the words used in the previous round. Kristen said she was going to concentrate on the new words instead. She felt comfortable spelling all the others.

When Kristen called us from school immediately after the spelling bee, I could tell the outcome from the tone of her voice.

"Dad, I lost," she said, fighting back tears.

"That's okay, sweetheart, I'm still proud of you."

"How could you be proud of me?" she asked.

"Just tell me one thing, Kristen, did you do your best today?"

"I think so."

"Well, if that's the case then I'm proud of you, and you have nothing to be ashamed of," I said. "Now, tell me what happened."

"I finished third," she said. "I spelled a word [candlewick] correctly, but one of the teachers didn't hear me. So I had to spell it over again and I left out the 'E'."

She started to cry, but I shook my head at her. "Crying's not going to help anything, is it?" I asked.

"No, Daddy."

"Tell me this, Kristen: Did you congratulate the winner?"

"Yes, sir."

"That's good. I think this whole experience will serve you well, Kristen, if you learn from it. You'll know you have to prepare a little better the next time and study all the material, the old words and the new ones (candlewick had been on the earlier list of words).

"But just because you didn't win today doesn't mean you failed. You were willing to go out there and compete. You took the risk. That shows a lot of character on your part. Don't let this one setback discourage you. Remember the pain and disappointment you feel right now and move forward.

"The next time, it might be your turn to win. Just remember that you took third place in the entire fifth grade. That's outstanding. Mommy and Daddy are proud of you for what you've accomplished."

3. Tell the Truth

Believe me, I know all about this lesson of life. When I was young, I had a penchant for prevarication. I don't know if my storytelling stemmed from a seed of mischief or a hyperactive imagination, but I could tell lies as expertly as some kids can jump rope. My older brothers and sisters didn't have to go to Burger King to get a whopper—they just needed to hang around me for awhile.

As I frequently remind my children, there's never an appropriate time to tell a lie. "But, Dad, I thought if I told the truth you were going to get mad," they have told me on occasion. Or they might say, "But, Dad, if I told the truth I knew I was going to get in trouble."

"Well, you've now gotten in more trouble by not telling the truth," I'll respond. "Look, when you lie, basically, you're taking a shortcut. When you lie, you're not showing any courage. You're being disobedient. In the short run, by telling a lie you might get away with something. But a lie is only a temporary solution to any problem. In the long run, the repercussions are so great. You can't sleep at night and you won't have any peace. Your whole existence won't be in harmony."

Whatever else you do, I remind our children, strive to tell the truth. Because whenever you lie, it begins to build a wall between us.

4. Be Humble

We try to teach our kids not to toot their own horns. If they do something special or exceptionally well, we're the first to congratulate them. We smother them with praise. But we don't want them walking around strutting like peacocks. We don't want any demonstrations of conceit or vanity.

We want our kids to know it's God who has given them the gifts and talents to use for his glory. We say, "He could have given those gifts to someone else, but he chose you instead. Be humble and appreciative for the gift. If you're going to boast about anything, boast about God."

5. Life Isn't Fair

"Life isn't fair." We hear this phrase all the time. I've said it, my kids have said it, my neighbors have said it—you've probably said it, too.

Take a look at the history of our country and the history of this world, and you'll see so many things that don't seem fair or just. Ask the Native Americans driven off their land to the reservations or the African-Americans brought to this country and placed into slavery and exploited. Ask people born in communist countries or under apartheid in South Africa, or living in Bosnia and Serbia.

How fair is it that professional athletes make more money than educators, social workers, and others who provide such vital service? How fair is it when the guilty go free?

No, it's not fair when good, committed parents have kids who rebel or when Christians try to do everything the right way and things still go sour. It's not fair when innocent infants arrive in this world addicted to crack cocaine and other drugs.

Too many bad things have happened to too many good people to make anyone but the most hopeless optimist think life is fair. Still, don't surrender to what you perceive as unfairness. Respond to it. Accept adversity as a given, learn from your setbacks, and move forward.

Fight the urge to play the victim or point the finger of blame at others. Rise above all that, and make a 100-percent commitment to making a difference with your life. God has given you that opportunity.

6. Be Responsible for Your Choices

We've evolved into a society that likes to blame others—not ourselves. When's the last time you heard someone say, "That was my mistake" or "I was wrong"?

We need more people like former President Harry S. Truman, who declared, "The buck stops here." He was willing to take the heat.

I can recall sitting in a film session with my defensive teammates during the 1984 season. Buddy Ryan ran back one play where we had all looked pretty foolish and disjointed and where we had given up big yardage. He asked Dan Hampton what had happened.

"It wasn't my fault, coach," shrugged Dan. "I had two men on me. I couldn't make the play."

Buddy started going around the room.

"McMichael?"

"Coach, I was being held," said Steve.

"Perry?"

"Wasn't my fault, coach," said The Refrigerator. "They had three guys blocking me."

"Defensive backs?"

"We couldn't hear Mike's call, coach."

Buddy had heard enough. He snapped off the projector and turned on the lights. "Guys," he said, "we're never going to be any good until we admit our mistakes and take responsibility for them," he said. "Nobody likes mistakes, but they happen. So admit them. Take ownership in them. Don't try to pass them on. I know you guys want to have ownership in all the glory when things are going good. Well, you have to take ownership in the mistakes when things don't. Never mind all the talent we have in this room, we'll never be champions until we can learn to admit our failures."

The following week, when Buddy turned on the projector, and starting going over plays, guys began speaking up immediately. "It was my fault," said one. "No, it was mine," argued another. "I was out of position. I should have been over there . . ."

I looked over at Buddy and I could see he was smiling, something he rarely did. He knew his guys had gotten the message. He knew our defense was ready to play together as one. We'd triumphed over the blame game.

In today's society, everybody's quick to blame the other guy. Or the system, the economy, the government, the color of their own skin. When you take responsibility for your mistakes and ask God to give you ownership in them, you'll be free to grow.

7. Lead by Example

Your actions speak louder than your words. Many people are filled with good intentions, but how many fail to back up the sentiments they express? Too many.

If you want to have friends, be a friend. If you want to be loved, be loving. If you want your children to treat others with respect, so must you.

I can recall raising my voice in anger at Kristen over what I knew was a petty incident. No big deal. I could tell right away that I had hurt her feelings, although she insisted that wasn't the case.

"Sweetheart, Daddy will make mistakes and screw up," I said, wrapping her in a hug. "That's part of being a dad. But I never want to feel better at your expense. I don't want to hurt your feelings, and I don't want you to build up walls of resentment.

"Any small hurt can grow into a big one when you don't let others know how you feel. So never hold things in. Let me know how you feel."

8. Have Courage

Whenever I'm asked to speak to youth groups, "have courage" is one message I stress. Why? Because it takes courage for a youngster to say no—no to drugs, no to premarital sex, no to other temptations—when their friends and peers are saying yes and trying to get them to go along.

And it takes courage for a youngster to say yes—yes I will follow the Lord, yes I will try to follow his path—when he sees his friends and peers paying no heed to the Holy Word.

Courage basically amounts to making the decision to do the right thing, regardless of the consequences or outcome. Courage is being willing to stand alone in the face of being excluded or ostracized. Courage is showing followers how to become leaders by stepping up and doing what's right. No matter who gets hurt.

9. Live Your Dreams

Kim and I want our children, even as young as they are, to begin thinking in terms of answering these kinds of questions: What do I want to accomplish in my life? What contribution can I make to this world? For what special purpose did God create me? What plan does he have in mind for me?

Each of us has been blessed with special gifts and talents. These gifts may range from fields like science and engineering to communication or problem-solving skills. They might be found in music or art or medicine—the list is endless.

If we're fortunate, we are able to identify our gifts and develop them to their fullest. Sadly, we all meet many people in life who have ignored their gifts or refused to honor them.

I discovered at a fairly young age I had a gift for playing football. "Hey, this is fun stuff," I told myself at my first practice, scarcely realizing at the tender age of thirteen that football would provide the means for earning a college education and become my first professional career.

I loved running into people at full speed and knocking them silly. I wasn't the biggest or strongest kid in school—in fact, for years I was a runt, the smallest guy among my peers. People still come up to me today and say, "Man you're not that big. Was that really *you* out there playing middle linebacker with those wild eyes?"

How does a person identify his or her gift? How can parents help their children in the discovery process? One way is by matching interests and aptitudes. Simply put, experiment with different activities and determine what you enjoy most and do the best. Then follow your dream by developing your gift.

I've read articles about two famous contemporary musicians, Ray Charles and Willie Nelson. Early on, people told them they couldn't sing a lick, that they'd be foolish to pursue a career in music. They each have sold millions and millions of records. Neither one listened to the naysayers and dream-busters.

Young people, like adults, need dreams to pursue. Too many kids live day to day, just going through the motions. Without dreams, without a plan to turn them into reality, children are at risk.

To my way of thinking, dreams are like bridges and visions are the cars we drive across the bridge. Making a plan of action represents the gas that fuels the car, and executing the plan represents pushing the gas pedal down and speeding ahead.

One last thing about dreams: I recently heard a remarkable story about actor Jim Carrey's dream. Several years before his career took off and he became a box-office favorite, Carrey wrote a check to himself for the princely sum of $10 million.

He put the check in his wallet and carried it around with him for years, watching as it became ragged around the edges.

Writing that check represented Jim Carrey's way of visualizing his dream of becoming such a major Hollywood star that one day a movie studio would offer him that staggering amount for his acting services. Sure enough, after the success of the Ace Ventura movies and *The Mask*, Jim Carrey reached the $10 million salary level. In fact, he far exceeded it.

When his father passed away, Carrey placed the check inside his dad's coffin as a final tribute to the man who had inspired and encouraged him.

10. Respect Yourself

By the way some kids dress and talk, it's easy to observe that they have no respect for themselves, much less for other people (especially their elders).

Gangsta rap music preys on this lack of respect and dignity. These talented young people could do a lot of positive things to change attitudes and perceptions in the inner city. They could instill some much-needed pride. Some of them do, but many instead choose to glamorize sex, violence, and drug use. It's a shame.

For your children to have self-esteem, they must first respect themselves and judge themselves to be worthy. They must develop an appreciation for their specialness and uniqueness. Where do they acquire such feelings of self-regard in the first place? You can't buy self-respect at the corner drug store or at the outlet mall. You learn that attitude from concerned, loving parents.

Self-discovery is a never-ending process. It begins at the earliest stages of awareness and doesn't end until we've drawn our last breath. The older I get, for example, the more I learn about my heritage, which is part German, part Native American, part

Mexican, part African-American. The more I learn about my culture and heritage, the more I'm able to discern who I am.

Right now in America, with the fracturing and fragmentation of families, we have a generation of kids walking around who don't really know themselves. They don't know their family history, they don't know where they came from, they don't know about their grandparents or great-grandparents.

Somewhere along the way, the baton has been dropped.

Generation gaps exist. There's no communication between old and young. Families feud. Respect breaks down. Those are dangerous trends that must be reversed.

11. Expect the Best

Whatever you do, jump in expecting the best results. This attitude translates into confidence. Confidence translates into better performance. It's circular, like a self-fulfilling prophecy.

So many times, people set out to accomplish great things, but they don't believe in themselves. They expect to fail. The fear of failure paralyzes their actions and they don't put forth their best effort.

If you expect the best, you'll often achieve it. If you fail, get up and try again, because you know you're not a failure.

It's like I told Kristen after her spelling bee: "Don't worry about your classmates teasing you because you made a mistake and misspelled a word. You were up there willing to fail. You put everything on the line. Lots of those kids pointing fingers at you and teasing you didn't have the courage to get up before the class and try. It's easy to sit on the sidelines and criticize. Remember, by getting into the arena and taking the risk, you've gone farther than most are willing to."

12. Be Disciplined

When you know what needs to be done, do it. It's that simple.

I remember Buddy Ryan had a rule for the Bears when we were running wind sprints: we had to touch every line. You might be slow as molasses, out of shape, ready to heave, but Buddy didn't care so much about that as he cared that you finish each lap and touch the line.

That took discipline. So did doing all the reps on the weight machines when I was working out in the offseason. No one was there watching me. No one else would know if I decided to do nineteen bench-presses instead of twenty. But *I* knew. And I had the self-discipline to push that bar up a twentieth time, no matter how much it hurt.

Discipline is a mind-set. You learn what you have to do, you do it, and it becomes habit. Kim and I have been giving the kids some "walk-through" drills lately to help them know how to start each day. What they have to do to get a jump-start on each day.

Soon, we hope, those steps will become second nature. They'll do them automatically.

Discipline means stopping yourself from lighting that cigarette, cracking open that bottle of alcohol, stopping off at the porno store. It's doing what's right—and not wavering. Discipline is what gets a person refocused when they veer off-track.

So Much to Learn

These twelve lessons, by a long shot, don't exhaust the category. I'm sure anyone reading this book can create a list, equally as valid, of life lessons worth teaching their own children.

I do believe, however, that at the core of any curricula for children should be lessons about conscience. About ethics, principles, morals, and respect. About setting standards for behavior. About knowing right from wrong.

Some other basic lessons to impart to children center on keeping a positive outlook in life. About filling our hearts and minds with affirming, empowering thoughts. About believing in yourself. About putting family first.

It's ironic that in this so-called Information Age, with all the access we have to data and information, so many of us understand so little about ourselves. We have the Internet and all these new delivery systems for instant access to oceans of facts and figures, and yet so many of us are lost and bewildered about life in general.

Knowledge is collecting facts. Wisdom is having a plan for action, putting all that knowledge to work. Knowledge can be trivial, or even useless, if it doesn't lead to action.

Many dads don't know what to teach their kids. They wind up acting more like companions than mentors. They play the role of bankers—a place to go for money, but that's about it.

Other fathers play fast and loose with life lessons. In some pockets of our society, what dad has been teaching is get ahead at any cost: Beat the system. Screw the other guy before he screws you. Look out for number one.

These are Machiavellian fathers, who espouse that the end justifies the means. To their way of thinking it's perfectly legitimte to cook the books, offer the bribe, double-deal, renege, stall, delay, accuse, harass, and, if necessary, sue to the hilt. Whatever it takes, get the job done. And make sure you take no prisoners: Go for the jugular.

Those are *not* the right lessons for fathers to be trying to impart. It would be better to teach your children nothing than that.

CHAPTER 18

Parenting with PEP . . . and Consistency

Regardless of what life lessons you choose to teach your children, dads and moms need to approach parenting with PEP. The acronym PEP stands for Preparation, Enthusiasm, and Passion.

Preparation

Preparation begins with allocating time for your children and their activities. I was reminded of the need for preparation during a flight home from Phoenix in early 1997.

I found myself seated next to an account executive who spends most of his time on the road, servicing accounts. The income tax deadline was approaching, and as he shuffled some papers, which looked to be IRS forms, he said that in 1996 his expenses for business travel came to roughly $70,000.

That's a lot of nights out on the road, I observed.

Too many, he agreed. He then told me that all his travel had cost him his marriage. He said he was so consumed by work that he hadn't been able to be a parent to his children or a helpmate to his wife. He had been an absentee father and husband.

Even when he was home, he placed such a priority on his work that he was constantly breaking promises to his wife and children. If they wanted to go to a movie or out to dinner, he told them, "We'll do it next week; I have to finish some business." Before he knew it, next week turned into next month—and next year.

A series of family problems grew out of his inattentiveness. His wife finally got fed up and filed for divorce.

"Now I do things differently," he told me. "I get to spend two weekends every month with my children and those weekends are totally theirs. They call all the shots. I don't answer the telephone and I don't answer my pager. My time with them is non-negotiable." Then he added ruefully, "I'm just sorry I didn't have a life when my wife and children needed me most."

As I reflected on his situation, I realized that fathers whose work takes them away from home a great deal—like the account executive and me—need to communicate to their children *this time is reserved exclusively for you. You're special, you deserve my total attention. I'm not going to allow anything or anyone to interrupt us*. It's critical to get the message across that children will have their own special time.

Preparation not only relates to dad's allocating his time to be with mom and the children and planning what activities to share, but also to deciding what information to impart.

For example, Kim and I have been trying to prepare our children for resolving conflicts by teaching them the proper way to respond when another kid says something spiteful in the classroom or on the playground—something on the order of "You're ugly" or "You're stupid." A child's natural reaction, of course, would be to respond in kind: "Oh yeah? Well you're double ugly.... you're twice as stupid."

We've been teaching our children that anyone who says such harmful, hurtful things to them probably has problems in their own life and in their own home. More than likely, someone (probably a parent or guardian) has hurled those same insults at them.

"Show some strength and compassion in that situation," Kim and I tell our kids. "The other child obviously is in some pain. He's trying to download that hurt on you. Ask the other child what's wrong. If you've hurt his feelings with something you've said or done, then apologize. Be a friend. If you show him you care, maybe he won't ever speak that way again.

"But don't go through life reacting to what others do," we stress. "Know who you are and who you serve, and have the courage to do the right thing."

A Playground Confrontation

Although we try to teach our children how to respond when certain situations arise, we have to combine patience with preparation. Kids aren't going to get everything right the first time.

Our family was sitting at the dinner table not long ago and Matthew said, "Dad, I did something really great at school today."

"Fantastic," I responded. "Tell me about it."

"I stood up for Jill, just like you tell us to do. This kid on the playground hit her, so I went over and hit him. Clobbered him good," Matthew beamed.

"Hold on a minute," I said. "That's not really what I'm talking about. That's the right idea, standing up for your sister. But maybe instead of hitting him back, you and Jill should have gone to the boy and said, 'Don't do that. That's wrong. Hitting another person is wrong. You wouldn't want me to hit your sister, so don't hit mine. Please don't do that again.'

"And if it happens again," I continued, "then go tell your teacher or the principal. Or if it happens again and you face a confrontation where you have to do something, just grab the other kid, pin his arms, and hold him. Protect yourself, but if you can help it, don't fight.

"Whatever you do, son, you don't want to dish out the same thing that happened to your sister. As Christians, we want to strive to be Christlike. Try not to follow up one wrong by committing another one."

Reading the Keys

As a football player, I had a reputation for thorough preparation. I spent countless hours—more than Kim and our children would have liked—breaking down an opponent's films, learning to read their formations, and learning to know their tendencies in specific situations pertaining to down and distance.

By the time the opposing quarterback began calling signals, I could read enough "keys" to have a good idea what kind of play was coming next. I adjusted the Bears' defense accordingly, then stared at the quarterback, daring him not to change the play.

The same type of intense preparation is required for being a father. Kim and I talk constantly about each of our children and the signals they are telegraphing: Are they distracted? Is something bothering them? Do they feel all right? We're always looking to read the keys. You can learn so much just from body language.

A Brave and Mighty Warrior

Preparation, in the form of being able to read the keys of my children's behavior, let me know something was bothering Matthew when he came home from kindergarten several years ago.

He was moping around the house, keeping to himself. When I asked him what was wrong, he said a girl on the school bus had told him he was ugly.

"Well, what do you think about that?" I asked him.

"I don't know," he muttered.

"Well, let's go into the bathroom and have a look."

We stood together in front of the bathroom mirror. "Tell me what you see, Matt."

"I see me," he replied.

"No, what *else* do you see?"

"You, Daddy."

"No, Matt, look harder. What do you see?"

After several seconds of silence, he finally said, "I don't know."

"Son," I told him, "before you were born, your mother and I used to pray that God would bless us with a brave and mighty warrior. And he did. That's what you are. You are a brave and mighty warrior, son of the Holy God. And you're a Singletary.

"Anytime someone tells you that you have the wrong color hair or the wrong color eyes or the wrong color skin, just remember that is a lie from the pit of hell."

The next day, and for several days after that, Matt said to me, "Dad, can we go into the bathroom again?"

"Sure," I said. Why not?

We stood in front of the mirror again. "I am a brave and mighty warrior for a holy God," he shouted. He was really fired up.

"That's outstanding, son," I told him.

On other occasions, when he's angry or pouting or can't get his way, I'll tell Matthew to go take a look at himself in the bathroom mirror. When he comes out, I'll ask him what he saw.

He'll begin mumbling "brave . . . mighty" in a low voice, almost a whisper, before I interrupt.

"Better go look again, Matt," I'll say. "You sure don't sound like a brave and mighty warrior." The next time he comes out, he can say those words with purpose.

We all need to be reminded that we are brave and mighty warriors, even if we don't feel that way at times.

Enthusiasm

Enthusiasm is another critical part of parenting. Dads must demonstrate enthusiasm for their children's activities, regardless of whether those activities are ball games, school plays, music lessons, scouting trips, or homework assignments.

For example, I started attending parent-teacher conferences several years ago. I've always been eager to meet my children's teachers and consistently disappointed by how few dads attend those meetings.

Ask dads to turn out for their children's soccer games on the weekend, and they'll be there. But extend them the opportunity to meet one-on-one with a classroom teacher, one of the most critical role models in their child's formative years, and they pass. They're too busy.

It's funny, even though dads can't be there, moms always manage to find a way to make the time. It's as if dads believe the recreational aspect of school is more important than the educational part. What kind of message is that?

Dad's enthusiasm for parenting cannot be feigned or faked. It has to be genuine. It can be, too, if dad immerses himself in his children's activities and realizes how valuable his contribution is to their growth.

I like to say that enthusiasm is as essential to any task, parenting included, as gasoline to an automobile. You can have the nicest car, with a great paint job and chrome all over, but if you have no gas in the tank, you're not going anywhere.

Making a Change

One of the most enthusiastic dads I know of is the father of a twelve-year-old boy in Dallas. This man is a devoted Dallas

Cowboys fan. He has followed the team for four decades, ever since 1960, when the Cowboys entered the NFL as an expansion team.

For most of his adult life, this man never missed a Dallas game on TV. He could tell you the name of every player on the Cowboys roster, what position he played, what jersey number he wore. He could tell you where that player went to college and, if he were married, the names of his wife and children.

He celebrated when Dallas won world championships in the 1970s under Tom Landry, and in the 1990s under Jimmy Johnson and Barry Switzer. His definition of a good year hinged on whether the Dallas Cowboys won the Super Bowl.

Then about a year ago, a light went off inside his head. As the father of a growing boy, this dad suddenly said to himself, "Why the heck am I sitting here on the couch, watching this football game on TV? Of what possible value is that to my son?"

Now the devoted Dallas fan spends his autumn Sunday afternoons with his son. They go to movies and museums. They play tennis and jump on the trampoline. They ride Dad's motorcycle along the back roads of East Texas.

The father still keeps up with how Dallas is doing in the NFL standings, even if he no longer knows which players are substituted in Cowboys' nickel package. But now he has become an expert on his own son's life.

Call that maturity and wisdom. Call that having the courage to make a change. I prefer to think of the Dallas fan's behavior as a shining example of establishing the right priorities and becoming an enthusiastic dad.

Cyberdad

I know of another father in Oklahoma who uses the Internet to create quality family time for himself and his three teenagers. This man is an accomplished photographer, one of the preeminent names in his niche. He spends roughly fifty percent of his time traveling nationally and internationally, often to faraway and exotic locations around the globe.

When he's away from home, he uses his laptop computer to send daily e-mail messages to the family. When he's home, he and his children surf the Internet, either in a general browse, learning more about the world and its inhabitants, or in a specific way, such as to complete homework assignments.

The family used the Internet recently to learn about the Great Barrier Reef in Australia and the Pyramids in Egypt. They've used it to plan vacations. The oldest child, who finishes high school in the spring of 1997 and enters college this fall, used the Internet to gather information on prospective colleges.

This dad and his children have used the Internet to explore the world together. It's been a valuable tool for the family, both educational and (relatively) inexpensive. It can be fun and informative—like having a public library in your own home. Most of all, the Internet serves to bring family members together in a shared activity that pays benefits to all.

As my children get older, I look forward to getting hooked up on the Internet and spending many hours surfing with my kids.

Passionate Dads

In addition to preparation and enthusiasm, dads need to bring passion to the parenting equation.

I've seen distance runners who could run fifty miles without stopping. I've heard of musicians who could practice eight hours a day with virtually no interruption. I know golfers who can beat balls all afternoon. I know of engineers and scientists who work all night in the lab or control room and do not miss their sleep.

Why? Because the activity they're engaged in represents their true passion. They feed off their own energy.

When you're doing anything with passion, time flies by. If you're doing anything without it, days drag. That could be a major problem for many American fathers: They don't exercise their gifts and talents. They settle for just having any job, just going to work, just getting by, without realizing their full potential.

The frustration fathers experience from not making an effort to fulfill themselves often turns to anger or indifference. Unfortunately, they bring that anger or indifference home from the job and inflict it on their spouse and children.

My passion for parenting can be seen when I pull out the little white board and a marker pen and start drawing examples about life for my children. I'm like a basketball coach drawing up formations and plays. I'll draw figures to represent family members and describe how they might react to different situations. What happens if we sin against God? What happens if we sin against each other? I'll ask the children to discuss the ideas and explain what the scenarios might be like.

My passion for parenting can also be seen in prayer. I frequently call Kim and the kids together for a family prayer. What's really exciting now is that my children have made prayer an important part of their daily lives.

We were getting ready to leave on a driving trip down to Texas last summer and as I was trying to shepherd everyone out of the house and into the van, one of the kids suddenly piped up: "Dad, we forgot to say our prayer."

Consistency

One of the most challenging parts of parenting, something easier said than done, is being consistent.

Inconsistencies can creep into the home like cockroaches into a kitchen and make a mess of things. Parents have to be diligent and work in concert so that dad doesn't tell the kids one thing and mom something else.

Kids are notorious for playing one parent off the other. I know, I used to try those things myself. If, for example, my father turned down my request for a trip to Baskin-Robbins, I'd go around to my mother and ask if she would take me.

Being consistent as parents requires a great deal of dialogue between dad and mom. You might not agree on every family issue, but when you speak to the children, it should sound like stereo: the same message coming from both speakers.

Drawing on personal experience, I'd like to share ideas for how to ensure parental consistency:

Keep the house rules clear and simple. It's unfair for parents to make children guess about expectations. For the kids' sake, and parents' consistency, write down what's expected of each family member. Keep the rules balanced and fair—and make sure everyone knows what's expected.

Stress individual differences. Some parents try to mold children with a cookie-cutter approach, forgetting that each of God's creations is special and unique.

As parents, we want to nurture the gifts and talents of each child. Such personal growth will be hindered if parents constantly compare one child with the other; by doing so, parents plant seeds of envy.

Recognize and limit the hypocrisy in your actions. It doesn't make much sense to tell your children one thing, then turn around and do something contradictory. I'm reminded of that public service announcement on TV where the father confronts his son after finding drug paraphernalia in the kid's room.

The dad accusingly asks, "Where did you learn that?" only to hear the kid reply, "From you, dad. Okay!?!"

I make a lot of noise around our house about keeping things neat. Obviously, I'm going to lose credibility with our kids if I insist they make their beds or pick up their clothes and I don't make my own bed and keep my clothes off the floor.

Keep your promises. You don't have to promise children everything (I strongly recommend you add the word "no" to your parental vocabulary), but when you do make a promise you must keep it. Kids are crushed and devastated when parents go back on their word. To them, it's the height of dishonesty.

Don't play favorites. I've heard parents praise one child and chastise another, right in front of them both. I've heard dads brag about one son and humiliate the other, to their faces.

I've seen on several occasions how fathers who played competitive sports favor their athletically gifted children over their nonathletic ones. That can be a damaging blow to a family and create serious tension between siblings.

Parents should try to extend praise and pass out hugs in equal measure. Strive your best to be fair, keeping in mind that uneven portions of affection or praise have potential for harm.

Speak the language of leadership. One of the ways parents can spark greatness in their children is by consistently employing the language of leadership.

Kim and I try to speak to our children with strong, empowering, affirming words. *Great, super, excellent,* and *terrific* are among our favorite adjectives. "You're the best," we'll tell them, "that's a terrific job."

My favorite word of affirmation is "outstanding." When the kids do a great job, I'm not the least bit bashful about telling them. I never want our children to think about just doing a job, or just getting by. Excellence should always be their goal.

We have another rule around the house: Never use words like *stupid, dumb,* or *ignorant.* Certainly not at the expense of someone else's feelings.

How many children in our society have had their development stunted and outlook dimmed because, at an early age, they were told they were stupid, ugly, or worse? Those words aren't part of the vocabulary in the language of leadership. They have no place in a household that is marching forward triumphantly.

CHAPTER 19

The Crossroads

Many dads today probably find themselves in the same situation I was in a few years ago. They are trying their best to be good husbands and fathers and making a sincere effort to provide family stewardship. They are raising their children with a blend of parental love and discipline, which represent the "Axe and Anchor" of fatherhood.

The Axe refers to self-esteem, honor, dignity, and character, tools that children (especially teens) can wield to chop away fears and doubts that influence their behavior. The Anchor refers to courage and conviction, which allow children to make good decisions about participating in gangs, cults, or other forms of rebellion.

Children armed with an axe can cut themselves free from the crowd that wants to experiment with drugs, alcohol, tobacco, and premarital sex. Parents who provide an anchor will give their children the foundation to help them stand on their own and not rely on peer groups to make their decisions.

These children won't be swept up in the tide of the times, nor will they be willing to just go with the flow. They aren't going anywhere they shouldn't.

Getting Nowhere with God

Some of these dads might also be reaching a contemplative state, where they grope for answers to life's major questions:

Am I doing the right things? Am I using my gifts and talents? Am I making a difference? Does my family feel loved unconditionally?

That was me a few years back: full of questions and in need of answers. I was desperately seeking to establish an identity apart from football and also trying to fill my role as a husband and father.

I was reading the Bible more frequently, saying more prayers, making more public appearances for organizations like Athletes in Action and Fellowship of Christian Athletes. I was racing about, spending too much time on the road, trying to build up brownie points with my Savior.

"Okay, Lord," I would say to him each night, "I'm doing this for you. I'm doing that for you. I mean, I'm all over the place for you, trying to spread your message and deliver your Word. That's gotta count for something, doesn't it?"

Finally, I heard a voice speak to my heart. "No, son, that's not it. You can't earn salvation. It's all about grace."

Some of us dads still have to learn that lesson. The fortunate ones are those who realize there is no way in the world to earn salvation. Rather, it comes when your heart is humble and when you've grown weary of trying to do things your own way. Salvation comes when a man or woman finally hits the wall and admits to needing something more in life than what they already have.

Salvation is transmitted through grace. Grace provides the means by which we enter God's kingdom and enjoy life everlasting. Grace, and grace alone, is the conduit. Grace is the only way.

When the Lord spoke to me and said, "Son, you can't earn it," I suddenly began to understand what Paul meant in Romans, chapter 7, when he wrote: "I do not understand what I do. For what I want to do I do not do, but what I hate I do. . . . What a wretched man I am! Who will rescue me from this body of death?"(vv. 15, 24).

The answer is clear: God will save you. Through grace, he already has. He did so on Calvary. Everything I need to go forward in life—as a father for my children, as a loving husband for my wife—was left behind long ago on that blood-stained cross.

I don't care what your character is, I don't care how many sins you've committed, if you will take your sins to the cross, God will say to you, "My grace *is* sufficient."

When I look back on those times of fatherly doubt and confusion, I know now why I was so frustrated and why I felt defeated in my Christian walk. I realize now that God has declared not everyone who calls out his name—not everyone who says "Hallelujah" and "Amen" and does all the "right" things—will enter his kingdom.

But those of us who accept him as Savior and Lord, will. Matthew 7:21 says, "Not everyone who says to me, 'Lord, Lord' will enter the kingdom of heaven, but only he who does the will of my Father who is in heaven."

I practically wore myself out trying to earn God's salvation. When you get to the point where you don't know what to do next—and despite having people all around, you still feel alone—*then* you'll be exactly where God wants you to be. At that point, you've reached a crossroads.

Get off the road of trying to be good enough. Get on the expressway where you accept him and surrender your will to his.

Allow God to work his will through your life and you will receive God's grace by faith. You will have your own relationship with him. He will guide your actions as a husband and father.

I know some fathers feel unwanted and unworthy. Some dads harbor feelings of not being valued. Some have been brainwashed into thinking that they have no right to do great things.

That's not true. God has a plan for every man's life. God has created every man to be a champion. The death of his Son Jesus Christ on the cross allows men like you and me to be victorious.

I know some readers of this book are still trying to earn their salvation. They are trying to do the right thing and trying to build up credits with good deeds. Sometimes, though, they feel that they're beating their head against a wall. I know, I've been there.

Let me say this again: a man can't go to church enough or sing enough hymns. He can't write out a big enough check. Until a man comes to the conclusion that he needs a Savior, that he needs Jesus Christ, everything he does will be vain.

When I think about the figure of Jesus hanging on the cross, I see the ultimate expression of character and integrity. Here is a man who came to earth and gave his all for humankind. Here is the man who took away my sins. Here is the man who knew me through and through—and still loved me. Unconditionally.

Every sin that I've committed, every sin that I've yet to commit, is on that cross. And because of his grace, I have the opportunity to be complete. I can be whole.

I pray that at some point fathers across America will rise up and ask, "Lord, what will you have me do?" Because God has the wisdom to enable fathers to prepare a new generation.

I also pray that fathers, when they feel exhausted by all the burdens and their feelings of inadequacy as family leaders, will look to the cross for comfort and inspiration.

May God bless us all.

CHAPTER 20

Success as a Father

Contrary to prevailing attitudes in America, I don't believe the success of any man, especially a father, should be equated with his wealth, status, or power.

In my book, a man's success has nothing to do with material possessions—who acquires the most elaborate and expensive toys, who is chauffered to work in a limousine, who owns a second home on a golf course—and everything to do with developing character, principles, and integrity and exhibiting leadership through service.

Maybe I'm in the minority on this, but I believe success (like beauty) comes from the inside. Success is reflected by whether we love ourselves and our families and whether we are kind and compassionate to the people we encounter along life's journey.

Misplaced Values

Somewhere along the way, we Americans got our values all messed up. Our culture, which exalts greed and pride, has distracted us from the most important aspects of life. The term "good family man," which should be among the highest of accolades anyone could receive, has become something of a stigma.

Instead of being considered heroes, good family men—those fathers more committed to nurturing their wife and children than building empires—are thought to be hopelessly out of step with the times. That's how crazy and off-base modern thinking has become.

Regrettably, many fathers consumed with career achievements and climbing the so-called ladder of success have bought into the myth that success equates with the size of a home or how much money is socked away, not how much love and laughter fills your household.

I beg to disagree. Did making All-Pro in the National Football League ten times qualify me as a success? No. Neither did signing a multimillion-dollar contract with the Chicago Bears. Don't get me wrong, I'm proud of my accomplishments in football. But when I reach the end of my life, I know all the honors and awards, and even that Super Bowl ring, will not be important.

What will matter most is how I chose to live my life. Did I honor and obey my parents, respect my brothers and sisters, love Kim unconditionally, raise our children carefully and caringly, honor others, hold to my convictions, and exemplify courage? Did I refuse to bow to the pressure of public opinion or what society deems to be politically correct?

If the answers to those questions are affirmative, then my time here on earth can be considered well spent. Because, quite simply, the essence of life is what you give—not what you get.

If I serve my family and friends and make a contribution to their well-being, I'll be an unqualified success, regardless of what others may say.

Regrets in Life

Speaking of all the American men handcuffed by materialism, I recently heard someone repeat the saying that never in history has a dying father uttered the words "I wish I had spent more time at the office."

Instead, dads on their death bed typically confess, "If I had it to do over, I'd want to spend more time with my kids. I'd get to know them better. I'd play more of a central role in their lives. My biggest regret is that I didn't do more for them than provide food, shelter, clothing, and an education."

Sadly, many dads fail to grasp that their responsibility as a father goes far beyond providing material goods. Dad's job is to be a leader and spiritual guide.

A father, in essence, is planting seeds for generations to come. If he blesses the members of his family, his seeds will be blessed. He will create a legacy of love that will span decades.

A loving relationship with his children is within any father's grasp. Children naturally reach out for daddy's love and affection and will continue to reach, unless his indifference, callousness, or tyranny, pushes them away.

I can't think of one valid reason for any man, anywhere, to become one of those rueful fathers who realizes, too late, that he wasted precious time he might otherwise have spent with his family. Dads need to make a full-time, emotional investment before their children become disengaged teenagers or estranged adults.

If a man is hungry for success—and most men are—the best place to try to achieve it is in the home, as a father.

Measuring Success

I've often been asked how fathers can determine whether they're doing a good job. That's easy. To measure his performance, a dad doesn't need to bring in an outside auditor or pollster. He can ask the people most qualified to rate his efforts—mommy and the children.

I'm aware I could do a better job as a father. It's something I strive to accomplish day and night. But it's comforting and assuring, when Kim and I gather our children together for family time, to hear them say things like:

"We know you and Mommy love each other very much."

"We like the way you play with us and spend time with us."

"Thank you for listening to us."

Hearing statements like those from my children's lips not only makes Kim and me feel good, it confirms that we're doing our job as parents. It's our report card.

Another way for a dad to determine his success quotient is to become a keen student of his children and their behavior. Be sure to study carefully such things as body language, how kids interact with others and what they say about themselves. You can tell in a heartbeat if children have good self-esteem. Or if they feel loved.

The answer to how dad's doing as a father is no mystery. Along with pigtails, freckles, wide eyes, and the gap that prompts the tooth fairy's visit, it's right there before his eyes.

The Best Dad I Know

I've known several men I consider great fathers, but perhaps none who was a better or more devoted dad than Sparky Beckham, one of my business partners. Sparky, who's now in his sixties, set a great example as a father—and now as a grandfather—by always keeping his children at the center of his focus.

Sparky and his wife, Merrie, raised a handful of great kids. I'm sure the Beckham family had its share of troubles and squabbles along the way—all families do. But I've yet to witness a warmer, more loving, and more loyal family atmosphere.

The Beckhams, who live in Dallas, are a close-knit clan. They have such a good relationship that Sparky's and Merrie's kids (now in their thirties and forties) frequently come over for dinner, or just drop in to chat. They all look forward to gatherings on Sundays and holidays. Thanksgiving and Christmas, two occasions that many families dread, are special celebrations.

Various members of the Beckham family attend church services together. They are a living example of that old saying that "the family that prays together stays together."

Every one of Sparky's five children—and his grandchildren—has been blessed by Sparky's unwavering love and devotion to family. They are a joy to behold.

Other Great Dads

I've met some other great dads through professional sports. My Chicago Bears teammates Les Frazier and Danny Rains are men who devote countless hours to supporting their children's activities. They invest time in their families, and when you're around the Frazier or Rains children, you see the dividends.

Their kids are well-mannered, respectful and fun to be around. They don't pout, whine, or act like spoiled children. You can see the balance of love and discipline in their young lives.

Another committed father I know is All-Pro Reggie White of the 1996 world champion Green Bay Packers. Reggie's one of the fiercest warriors ever to step onto a football field, but away from the game, he's more concerned with fatherhood than fame.

Years ago, when Reggie played for the Philadelphia Eagles, he took quite a ribbing from some of his teammates for not going along with the crowd. The Eagles had some rowdy guys back then, but when the partying started Reggie was nowhere to be found.

Some of the Eagles used to call Reggie hen-pecked (actually, they used stronger language) and teased him for being such a stay-at-home kind of guy. But Reggie, to his everlasting credit, has always been a pillar of strength for his family.

Another great dad is baseball's Tim Burke, whom I met through Pro Athlete Outreach (PAO). At the peak of his career with the Los Angeles Dodgers, Tim decided to retire, devoting himself to his five adopted children. I have to admire Tim for the strength of his convictions and for making a "family first" decision. A lot of sportswriters around the country thought Burke was nuts for walking away from his livelihood, but he heeded a higher calling.

As I've mentioned several times, Kim grew up in a loving home. At the head of that family is a man who was—and is—wild about his five children. My father-in-law, Donald Courtley, made many sacrifices for his family. Put them all together and they spelled L-O-V-E.

I thank God for the loving example Kim's father set. It has provided so much of the foundation for our own growth as a family.

Invest the Time, Dad

What makes Sparky Beckham, Reggie White, Tim Burke, Donald Courtley, and the other successful fathers I've mentioned such great dads? The investment they make in their children. Many fathers fail in that regard.

I speak frequently to youth groups at high schools and churches or through organizations such as the Fellowship of Christian Athletes and Boy Scouts of America. I enjoy those appearances a great deal, because they allow me to keep a finger on the pulse of America's kids.

Sad to say, I've lost count of the number of times teenagers have told me, "I wish I could see my dad more, but he's always at work" or "I wish my dad could come to some of my games, but he's too busy." And—this one really stings my soul—many times teens have confided, "I wish I knew if my dad thinks I'm special."

It's troubling that so many kids walk around with insecurity and doubt, often because fathers have failed to let them know they are special, valued, and loved.

Giving Your All

We're currently making plans to build a new house next year. We want to downsize from the large, three-story home we occupy. We don't need as much space now that Kim's grandparents, who lived with us for several years, have moved to Tennessee.

Before talking with the builder about plans for the new house, Kim and I came to the conclusion that we want our children to share bedrooms. We want each of them to have their own accountability partner, someone to make sure they keep their area clean and pick up their clothes. We don't want any child isolated from the family.

Kim and I like the togetherness that comes from sharing a bedroom. So do the children.

We'll probably design the house with extra space in the kitchen and dining areas. That's where we congregate as a family and enjoy most of our family time.

One day when I was out driving around the area, looking at residential property for the new house, I came upon a cemetery. On impulse, I pulled the van over to the side of the road and let the engine idle while I looked at the gravesites.

Some of the markers were impressive slabs of marble and stone. The sheer size of the monuments denoted wealth, status, and power. Others headstones were small and understated.

As I sat there, I began thinking what words or numerals would look good on my headstone, besides my name and the dates of my existence. Perhaps my uniform number for the Chicago Bears? The words All-Pro or Middle Linebacker? Maybe my nickname (Samurai)?

I decided the highest accolade any man could receive on his headstone would be the words "Good Husband and Loving Father."

Then I remembered something that Mel Farr, the former star running back for the Detroit Lions once told me. I can't remember how the topic came up in conversation, but Mel, who now owns several Ford dealerships in Michigan, said, "Mike, when I'm gone I want my tombstone to read 'Here Lies Nothing.'"

"Why would you want that?" I asked.

"Because I want to give everything I have while I'm here on earth," he said. "I want to use it all up. If I'm going to accomplish all I'm supposed to as a man, there won't be any left over."

I moved the gearshift into drive and slowly pulled away from the cemetery, taking one last sideways glance. I think Mel Farr was right: I want to give Kim and our children everything I have to offer—love, wisdom, support, encouragement, consolation, affirmation. Like Mel Farr said, I want to use it all up.

If I give my all to my family, I'll be making a great investment for eternity. It's an investment that ensures I will have been a success as a husband and father.

CHAPTER 21

New Priorities and a Positive Approach

At seminars and corporate training sessions, I often ask audiences to rank these five categories in order of importance in their lives: family, career, friends, personal development, and spiritual development.

Many participants, though by no means all, rank family first. Some are being sincere, but some probably do so because they think that particular response is the "right" answer. A large majority of the respondents put careers second, behind family. Some people even rank careers first.

I often ask these audiences to describe what the world would be like if we really meant what we say about our families being most important. That is, if our actions matched up with our sentiments. It wouldn't be a perfect place, of course, but as a society we'd be light years ahead of where we are.

I'll remind audiences, though, that if we inspect our calendars and checkbooks—and examine where we spend our time and money—we'll know whether we indeed put family first. To be blunt, many people pay lip service to family matters but succumb to selfishness.

As I noted earlier, that description fit me at the outset of our marriage. Fortunately, Jesus Christ became a central figure in my life. That, together with Kim's love and patience and my mother's counsel (and prayers from them both) turned me around as a father.

Rearranging Priorities

I hope this book inspires some readers, dads and moms alike, to change priorities and make family considerations the center of attention. I believe building God's kingdom is—or should be—parents' primary mission here on earth. I know I'm not the only father who shares that point of view.

The first step in setting a new agenda as a father or parent is to have a vision for where you want your family to be tomorrow, next week, or five years from now. Personally speaking, I want our children to be going forward in every phase of their lives, growing up and maturing, thirsting for knowledge, taking risks, daring to be great, and becoming bold witnesses for the Lord.

Once this vision for a family exists, parents should confer about what steps are necessary to ensure such growth. Chances are, they will conclude the most critical variables in their children's development are (a) having a close relationship with dad and mom; (b) receiving a substantial investment of dad's and mom's time; (c) living a disciplined life within boundaries; (d) accepting personal responsibility; (e) receiving unconditional love; (f) having a personal relationship with Jesus.

(I'd submit that two other important variables are how many hugs and kisses children receive and how often they hear the affirming language of leadership.)

Once dad and mom make those determinations, and a game plan is fixed and agreed upon by everyone—including the children—a family can move ahead toward maximizing its potential.

Making Changes with God's Help

Some dads probably possess a desire to be better fathers, but don't know how. They are unable to shake off negative influences that inhibit their ability to provide leadership in the home.

Some fathers might be working in careers that yield little satisfaction, performing jobs in perfunctory fashion without passion. These dads bring home with them each day an attitude of defeat, discouragement, and distress. Their unhappiness permeates the household and damages relationships with mom and the children.

These dads seem to be stuck on a treadmill. They either feel like they're running in place, going nowhere, or that they're running a race without any idea of when or where they'll reach the finish line. Many dads are just going through the motions of living, lacking purpose and direction.

It's not a hopeless situation, however. If I can change as a father—as hard as it was—they can, too.

These dads can make changes, starting by removing themselves from negative surroundings. They might begin, for example, by switching career directions, getting a different job, or moving into a line of work that's more rewarding and fulfilling. Most of us can cite examples of men we've known who were frustrated in one career but found peace and happiness after starting another.

My Friend Bob

I have a friend named Bob who was growing increasingly frustrated at work. He repeatedly met resistance to his ideas for moving his firm (which specialized in graphics and printing) forward. The managers above him didn't want to assume the risk. They were fearful of innovation and change.

Bob became labeled as something of a rebel within the company. The promotions he sought went to yes-men on the payroll—those who never rocked the boat. Bob felt thwarted and miserable, even though he remained a top performer in the firm.

Finally, Bob decided to go into business for himself. He used his contacts and expertise in the graphics and printing business to set up his own firm. He was able to put his innovative ideas to work.

Bob, like me, is the father of six children. Being his own boss, he now has more time to devote to his family. He's much happier in every facet of his life, personally and professionally. His family has been rewarded because Bob was willing to change his environment.

Sometimes, though, men express a desire to make changes in their life but take no action. They remind me of record albums with the needle stuck in a groove, droning on and on about how they intend to change—without doing anything about it.

They frequent the same bars or hangouts and keep the same group of friends. Their decisions stifle growth and change, but rather than accept responsibility for their actions—or inaction—they point the finger of blame at someone else. They blame their job, their boss, or members of their family—most often their spouse. Everybody but themselves.

How can this kind of man change as a father? One, by finding books or tapes that deal with the process of change. Two, by finding accountability partners who will keep him on track. Three, by developing prayer partners who will provide guidance and strength. Four, by studying the Word, setting aside a few moments each day for Scripture reading (God says that if you lack wisdom, ask him). Five, by finding a Bible-teaching church and continuing to pray.

Most important, these men must learn to take their troubles, concerns, and fears to the Lord. They have to ask God to come in and be the Lord of their lives. God is in business to answer prayers and help believers transform themselves. I know. I speak from experience.

Learning a Positive Approach

I wasn't always a positive, "can-do" type person. In fact, when I was a youngster, I was pretty much a goof-off and class clown. On more than one occasion, my elementary school teacher called me up to the front of the class because I was cracking jokes in the back of the room.

One of the most profound changes in my young life came when I discovered how essential it is to develop a positive attitude. Trust me, the power of self-belief is an incredibly strong one. I've spent the past twenty-five-plus years of my life proving that point.

Just as I entered my teens, I read a book by Dr. Norman Vincent Peale called *The Power of Positive Thinking*. Being introduced to Dr. Peale's philosophy had the same effect on me as an alarm has on a firefighter: I took immediate action and began moving in high gear. I felt a burning desire to succeed, and I realized from reading Dr. Peale that desire would carry me a long way toward my goals.

When I finished that book, I set it down and said to myself, "You can make a difference with your life, Mike. You can be somebody. The only thing holding you back is *you*."

At roughly the same time, my mother gave me a foundation of hope. She taught me stories from the Bible and inspired me with Scripture, including one of my favorite verses: "I can do everything through him who gives me strength" (Philippians 4:13).

Inspired by Dr. Peale and fortified by my mother's love and teaching, I became organized and focused. Basically, I reinvented myself. I was no longer the neighborhood cut-up, the little boy with few goals, low self-esteem, a wild imagination, and a loose tongue. I found a purpose for my life—playing football—and focused on developing my skills. I became a sponge, soaking up every bit of information I could.

I realized, at age thirteen, that if I set goals academically, put energy into football, and trusted the Lord and continued to pray, I could realize my potential as a human being.

Now, at age thirty-eight, I realize that if I have complete faith in the Lord and put my total energy into fatherhood, my children will realize their potential.

One of the best decisions I made in the aftermath of reading Dr. Peale's book was to sever ties with the group of guys I hung around with during our years in elementary school. Even at such an early age, those guys were showing signs of a reckless, dangerous life.

Someone with cataracts or double vision could have seen those guys were headed for trouble (which, sad to say, most all of them found). I knew I had break off those relationships or I'd be putting myself at risk. I cut the cord.

My Rankings

Let's come back full circle to the beginning of this chapter, where I mentioned ranking those five categories in life. When people ask me for my own rankings, I list spiritual development first, family second, and career third.

Some people in the audience invariably register surprise at hearing that. "You talk so much about family, Mike," they say. "I can't believe it's not first on your list."

I try to explain that if I put my relationship with the Lord first, everything else will fall into place. Because if I surrender my will to him and allow his will to work through me, I will be the kind of father my family needs me to be.

He made me. He knows my make-up, how I'm wired. Because he is my creator, he can guide me.

I don't believe that any man can truly lead his family, or love his wife and children, unless Jesus Christ is leading him. He will be unable to recognize that the battle he fights is a spiritual one.

If, however, he puts Jesus Christ first in his life and develops a personal relationship with him, he will become the kind of father he hopes to be. The kind of dad that his children will honor and respect.

Chapter 22

Taking a Look Back

While we were in the process of writing this book about fatherhood, I decided to contact several committed dads I had been fortunate enough to get to know. I posed this question to them:

"Looking back, if you had to do it all over, what would you do differently as a dad?"

Their responses were varied and revealing. Most all of them acknowledged they would have made some changes in their parenting, principally by investing more time and energy in the relationship with their children.

Several, however, pointed out that their children had turned out well.

Bill Glass, who runs a prison ministry service (and with whom I appeared at the Cook County Jail and the Texas state prison meetings mentioned earlier), wrote back in reply:

> First, I would bless more and teach less. No matter how much we teach [our children], if we don't bless them they struggle with insecurity for the rest of their lives.
>
> Blessing communicates three things. First, belonging. There would be no need for children to join gangs if they felt they belonged to that most important gang of all—the family. It is the father's job to make the child feel that he or she belongs.

Secondly, blessing communicates 'I love you.' You must communicate love by saying and doing those things that show it. Above all, a dad must look unblinking into the eyes of his children and wife and say it out loud while touching them: 'I love you.'

Thirdly, the blessing should include value. ('You are terrific. Not only because of what you do, but simply because of who you are.') It is important to compliment what children do and express appreciation for it, but it goes beyond that. Love must be unconditional, otherwise it is not love—it's a negotiation. So, it is important to communicate love that has nothing to do with what the child has done. Good or bad, right or wrong.

Bill Glass also offered this revealing observation:

> In the last twenty-five years, I have been in more prisons than any living human, and the thing that overwhelms me is how few inmates are really blessed. I am convinced that criminality grows out of a lack of the blessing of the father.
>
> On death row in Parchman, Mississippi, I asked every inmate, 'How do you and your dad get along?' I got forty-four negatives out of forty-four inmates. All of them hated their dad. There is something about it that makes a man mean when he doesn't get along with his father. One of the causes of criminality is no doubt a father problem.

Dr. Tony Evans, senior pastor of the Oak Cliff Bible Fellowship in Dallas, responded to my question by saying,

> If I had it to do over again, I would shield my wife better from the problems of ministry so that I would protect her from being overburdened by the needs of people. Coupled with this I would express, much more often than

> I have, the value and importance her gifts and talents have meant to me, my family and my ministry.
>
> With my children, if I had it to do over again, I would allow less ministry interruptions to interfere with our family time.

Do you notice a recurring theme? These fathers recognize that family time is precious. It's time to be treasured.

Zig Ziglar, the acclaimed consultant, motivational speaker and author of *Over the Top*, wrote,

> Chances are excellent the only thing I would do differently would be to add the word "more" in my relationship with my son.
>
> I like where my son is. He's a man of integrity with a clear, sharp mind, a good work ethic and excellent people-skills. He's functioning as the President and CEO of our company and is doing a marvelous job.
>
> Having said that, I would add "more" to the mix we used. I would spend even more time talking with him. I would spend even more time with him at night, reading Bible stories and sharing experiences of the day, inquiring more about what had been happening in his life. I would encourage him to read more of the good books, and I would read more of those good books to him, along with even more Bible reading. I would take him more places and introduce him to more people who would be great mentors, role models, and teachers; people with similar philosophies who have their feet on solid ground and who genuinely love young people.

That's a great word for all dads to add to their parenting: More.

Dr. James C. Dobson, who heads the popular worldwide ministry Focus on the Family and who is the author of several best-selling books about family issues, replied with a story about how fatherhood came into focus in his own life.

> I certainly made my share of mistakes as a father. Like millions of other men of my era, I had a tough time balancing the pressures of my profession with the needs of my family. Not that I ever became an "absentee father," but I did struggle at times to be as accessible as I should have.
>
> As it happened, my first book *Dare to Discipline*, was published the same week that our second child, Ryan, arrived. A baby always turns a house upside down, but the reaction to my book added to the turmoil. I was a full-time professor at a medical school, and yet I was inundated by thousands of letters and requests of every sort. There was no mechanism to handle this sudden notoriety. I remember flying to New York one Thursday night and doing seventeen television shows and press interviews in three days, then returning to work on Monday morning. It was nothing short of overwhelming.

Dobson then received some important counsel from his own father.

> My father, who always served as a beacon in dark times, saw what was happening to me and wrote a letter that was to change my life. First, he congratulated me on my success, but then he warned that all the success in the world would not compensate if I failed at home. He reminded me that the spiritual welfare of our children was my most important responsibility, and the only way to build their faith was to model it personally and then to stay on my knees in prayer. That couldn't be done if I invested every resource in my profession.
>
> I have never forgotten that profound advice. It eventually led to my resignation from the university and to the

> development of a ministry that permitted me to stay home. I quit accepting speaking requests, started a radio program that required no travel, and refused to do "book tours" or accept other lengthy responsibilities that would take me away from my family.
>
> As I look back on that era today, I am so grateful that I chose to preserve my relationship with my children. The closeness that we enjoy today can be traced to that decision to make time for them when they needed me most. I could easily have made the greatest mistake of my life at that time.

Dr. Dobson put his family first. His is an example all fathers can heed.

Norm Evans, a former NFL player with the Oilers, Dolphins, and Seahawks, now runs the Pro Athletes Outreach (PAO) from his home in the Pacific Northwest. PAO helps athletes with spiritual development and marital issues. Norm wrote,

> Thank you for asking me to reflect on what I would do differently in being a dad now that my children are thirty-four and twenty-nine years old, because it is never too late to start doing some things differently, and this process has encouraged me to start doing some things differently now.
>
> To top my list I would try to "lighten up." I tend to be a rule keeper . . . if a sign says don't walk on the grass, I don't walk on the grass—and I felt everyone else should not walk on the grass. But now I realize that God has given me much *grace*, and I am trying to learn to be grace-giver instead of a rule-giver. Now I believe that we as parents should have as few rules as possible and be sure we consistently enforce the few real important rules we set.

Along the same lines, I would be much more open and candid with my children about my own doubts, fears, failures, and feelings. When our children were small, I thought Dad should always *appear* in control. This appearance, or image, that I projected set a standard of performance that has hurt my children. I believe they felt like it was impossible to live up to my standards and discipline of life.

Now I try to express my fears and failures and tell them how I'm trying to work through them. I try to show them God has been loving and forgiving to me. I want them to know when and how I blow it and how I receive forgiveness and restoration. . . . My hope is that they will see how I resolve the core issues of my life. It would have been much easier to do when they were living at home.

If I could do it over again, I'd hug 'em more, kiss 'em more, laugh more, cry more, listen more.

If I could do it over, I'd eliminate shame and blame messages like "I'm very disappointed in you"; "Can't you *ever* do anything right?"; "Don't be so stupid." I would replace those *you* messages with "I feel sad about the decision you made"; "I feel scared about the influence that person can have on you"; "I feel angry because you didn't do what you said you would do."

When in doubt about what to say, I'd try to say, "I can't talk about this right now. I'm not clear what's going on inside me. I need to think it over." Or "I don't know the answer to that, but I'll get you an answer."

Then I'd learn how to ask more questions that couldn't be answered with one word. Instead of saying "How was your day today?" I'd say "On a scale of 1 to 10, how would you rate your day?" then "Tell me why you would give it that rating."

> Finally, I would try to understand my children's makeup. Are they introverted or extroverted, and what is the best way to communicate with them? Do they gather information by seeing, hearing, or reading? I'd try to learn their spiritual gifts and anything else I could in order to understand them better, and I'd try to be a servant in the home instead of a rule-giver.

There's a great follow-up story to Norm's letter back to me. Last Christmas, he put a copy of it in his children's stockings. On Christmas morning, in the middle of opening gifts, they read their dad's heartfelt words about fatherhood and togetherness.

The family shared hugs, kisses—and not a few tears. They decided that having a father who loves his children and is committed to them is truly one of life's greatest gifts.

We want to hear from you. Please send your comments about this book to us in care of the address below. Thank you.

ZondervanPublishingHouse
Grand Rapids, Michigan 49530
http://www.zondervan.com